AF473804

BRVEGEL

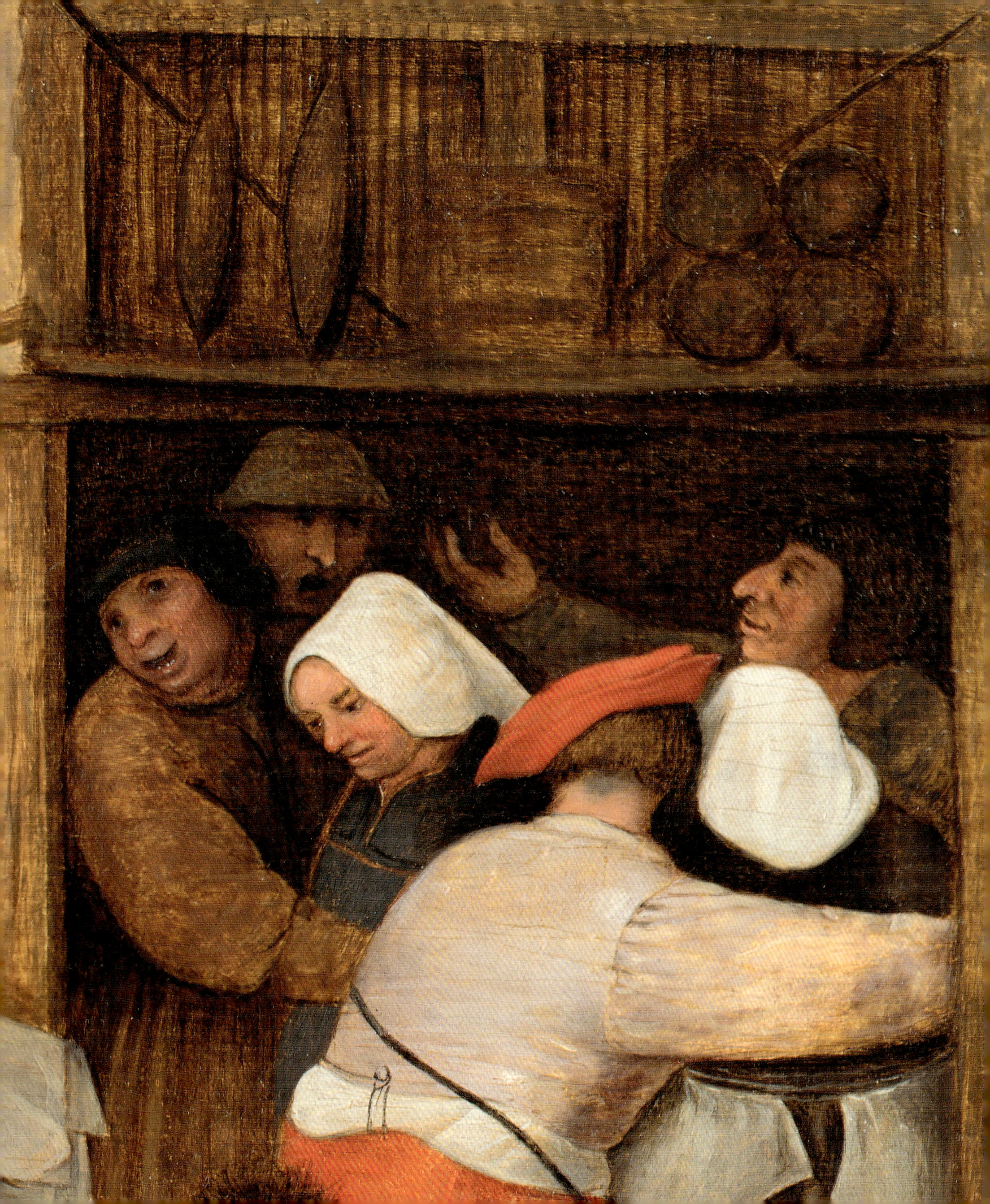

Dancing Peasants at a St. Sebastian's Kermis

A Rediscovered Painting by Pieter Bruegel the Elder

Maximiliaan P.J. Martens

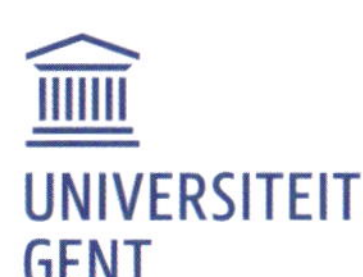

SilvanaEditoriale

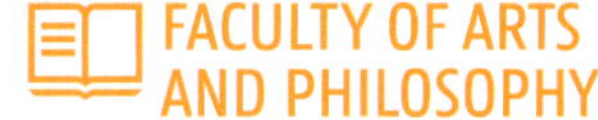

6
Preface
by dr. Paul Huvenne
EMERITUS GENERAL DIRECTOR - ROYAL MUSEUM OF FINE ARTS, ANTWERP

10
Introduction

12
Biography

A Rediscovered Painting

30
Iconography:
Peasants' Kermises in Bruegel's Oeuvre

36
Materials and Condition

45
Painting Technique and Stylistic Analysis

55
Provenance and Attribution

58
Endnotes

60
Literature

62
本书末页附有简介，生平和《起源与归因》一文。

Preface

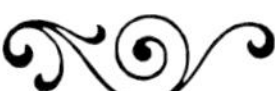

It seems as if Pieter Bruegel the Elder didn't hold the connoisseurs of his day in high regard. One gets this impression from the caricature-like depiction in the drawing *The Artist and the Connoisseur* at the Albertina in Vienna. Both men seem to be looking at a painting that is being made set off-screen on an easel. The artist with weary hair almost fills the whole sheet and holds the hilt, in this case a brush, firmly in his hand. He stares gloomy ahead with a dogged expression. The connoisseur behind him is positioned somewhat pressed towards the margin. He doesn't seem to be very empathic with his skimpy lipless mouth, plump nose and his owl's glasses. However, he is likely to pay good money for what he is shown.

Although most of what is depicted in this image leads to such a reading, it might perhaps be nothing more than *Hineininterpretierung*. Whatever both gentlemen may think of one another, one thing is obvious: the artist has to share his work with a connoisseur willing to pay for his art, who probably doesn't understand any of it, and only personizes theory with his comments. Nonetheless, the artist remains master of his brush and stands consciously and centrally.

The phenomenon of the connoisseur was relatively new in Bruegel's time and an immediate consequence of the intellectual emancipation of the fine arts throughout the humanist renaissance since the *Quattrocento*. During the Middle Ages – but also e.g. in Greek antiquity – artists had the status of artisans. The artist was a manual laborer who had learned his trade within an artisanal tradition. He knew how to make an image and was equipped with the necessary knowledge to talk about it. But he only did so with colleagues or when training pupils. The tricks of his trade remained his professional secrets.

As the attention for artisanal achievement shifted during the humanist Renaissance to art based on theoretical argumentation, the artisan became *artist*, whose endeavors were valued as equal to the seven liberal arts that formed the prolific basis for science. The trade of the image maker received the status of Fine Arts. As *pictor doctus*, its creator gradually became equivalent to the academic. The change in transferal of knowledge was crucial in this process as by the 17th century it was formalized in the academies, and as such positioned on an equal level of academic education.

An artisanal trade was handed down from Master to Master as an initiation in the secrets of the profession. This is by definition conservative, directive and protectionist. An academic discipline shares its knowledge and research in an open and free discourse. As a consequence, the professional is no longer the sole one competent to engage with art. He has to accept that also non-practitioners of his trade can judge his work.

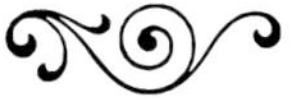

There can be little doubt that as a painter Bruegel was like his contemporary colleagues, equally familiar with the art theoretical insights of the Renaissance artist and connoisseur. Therefore, we hand the word to a connoisseur who proclaims why he admires Bruegel. Such an attempt can be easily made by turning to the praise expressed by Lampsonius for his friend Pieter: "*He was the greatest artist of his time*" or what Karel van Mander wrote about the master in his *Schilder-boeck* of 1604 (fol. 233r): "*Nature found and struck luck wonderfully well with this man only to be struck by him in turn in a grand way [...] He was wonderfully sure in his poses and he had a very pure and subtle technique with the pen with which he drew many small views from life...*"

Perhaps the connoisseur may insinuate that he is aware that Bruegel's compositions and figures are references to Titian or other Italian masters of the High Renaissance. Or perhaps he would like to elaborate on the idea of how through artists like Bruegel genre painting gained its place next to history painting in the art collections of his time and how those genre paintings had become the object of renewed art experience. Or does he express his sympathy for the way artists like Bruegel integrate vernacular culture in their inventions? This brought art as close to man as humanist Latin was remote to contemporary life and it incited much more of an authentic experience. Evidently, both men agree that the very essence of a work of art is still embodied in the concept and the invention of the image. The artist does sign his work with 'PIETER BRVEGEL INVENIT', doesn't he? But what about autograph execution?

It seems as if the artist is annoyed by the connoisseur, who with all his learning apparently knows better what he intends with his unsophisticated talent. After all, is he anything else than an artisan? The artist looks disturbed by all these pretentious comments and asks attention for the virtuoso execution of his discipline that allows him to be creative and to materialize his genius insights. It can be observed to what degree this is essential when one generation later Rubens draws free-handedly a perfect circle as his contribution to a *Liber Amicorum*. The emblematic importance of such a circle reappears in a self-portrait of c. 1665 by his colleague Rembrandt, where it functions both as background and attribute.

During the 17th century, art praxis becomes ever more academic, and along with this, connoisseurs collect art with increasing knowledge. The traditional *Kunstkammer* evolved into galleries. The aristocracy set the tone, and rich upper-class burghers followed their example. David Teniers II, who was related by kin to Bruegel, depicted the collection of Leopold Willem in his *Theatrum pictorium in quo extribuntur ipsius manu, eiusque cura in aes incisae picturae architipae iltalicae quas archidux in pinacothecam suam Bruxellis collegit* of 1660. It is noteworthy that the curatorship of such a large collection was still entrusted to a professional painter, but this didn't prevent collecting art from becoming a hobby, even some sort of sport. This is how the phenomenon of the *amateur curieux* originated, who with the writings of André de Félibien (1619–1695) and Roger de Piles (1635–1709) at hand, taught himself the names and styles of the artists he was supposed to know. In these texts he learned where to concentrate on, the so-called 'principles': invention, composition, expression, drawing, color, anatomy, proportions, perspective... and de Piles even provided charts in his *Cours de Peinture par Principes* (Paris 1708) to evaluate all this with marks. This is how connoisseurship became the very apex of the art world. To familiarize oneself with this, one had to study art theory and accumulate knowledge about stylistic evolution, as described e.g. by Joachim Winckelmann in his *Geschichte der Kunst des Altertums* (1764). The main goal for any connoisseur was to develop good taste. As such his questioning art became aesthetics, a branch of philosophical thought. Connoisseurship evolved not so much towards science but more as part of the art of living, more akin to leisure, to sports, be it top sports with high stakes. Not so much has changed in our days.

After the French Revolution the large European museums evolved into civil institutions entrusted to professional civil servants. Their business was conducted in a decent, reliable and verifiable fashion. However, the old skills and attitudes from the ancient régime still proved useful. Connoisseurship remained the preferential skill for cataloging collections and acquisitioning them. But parallel to history evolving towards a scholarly discipline in the wake of the natural sciences, the connoisseur in a museum became an art historian, who preferred to rely upon the historical context of the objects in the collection, and considered visual sources as tied in with the heuristics of written sources. This provides more certain knowledge and the debate about works of art was detached from non-committal aesthetic speculation. Art experience became enthralled in the certainty delivered by historical research. The (art)historically educated civil servant was so successful in the museum world that his judgement and vision reached the status of being inevitable in the estimation of a work of art.

The art historian searched for a better legitimation in using his connoisseurship. Two tendencies manifested themselves. The first relies upon an intuitive sense and is based upon some sort of synthetic thinking. Max Friedländer described in an unsurpassed fashion what that is all about in his very readable book *Von Kunst und Kennerschaft* (Oxford/ Zürich, 1946). It is a skill acquired by training: practice leads to perfection. Yet talent is required. He who has it, only has to reveal it. Among professionals this is known as 'having an eye'. It seems that Bruegel thought his companion with his thick eye glasses had it only to a rather moderate degree. Fritz Mayer van den Bergh did possess this intuition improved by practice when he first saw Bruegel's then unknown - and now beautifully restored - *Dulle Griet* (Mad Meg). When he bought it, he surpassed Friedländer, and his enormous talent became evident. Few colleagues have such an eye.

But the average art historian found the legitimation for his connoisseurship otherwise, methodologically much easier to master, for it is analytical and can therefore be followed step-by-step. The best-known example is the method of Morelli, although the *Kunstgeschichtliche Grundbegriffe* (Munich, 1915) by Heinrich Wölfflin also belongs to the same category. It witnesses a bourgeois hunger for certainty: there where connoisseurship abandons us.

Over generations, art history has become a scholarly discipline strongly influenced by historical methodology: a discipline that is taught at the best universities. Hessel Miedema explored the limits and possibilities of this discipline in a sharply written booklet, *Kunsthistorisch*.

The art historical knowledge is not only the product of museum professionals who have been invited to it by their daily engagement with works of art. The art market also needed to keep pace with this debate, and contributed enormously to art historical knowledge, even altering established points of view.

It is exciting to observe that within this evolution of the art historical discipline, the art work itself has increasingly claimed a central place as primary source in research. As any written source, the visual source has to be subjected to heuristic criticism. Questions are asked about authenticity, state of conservation, provenance, etc. This type of fundamental research invites further inquiry from an iconological, sociological, anthropological and cultural historical perspective.

With the arrival of the art historically trained curator in the museum world, the artist became increasingly oppressed. His knowledge and comprehension were wanted only when it comes down to conservation. But as a profession conservation/restoration has also undergone fundamental changes. Technical research on materials and increasing knowledge of the creative process have enlarged the field to such a degree that we are inclined to rename the discipline as 'art science'. One of the major consequences was that the visual observation became increasingly a reflection on the material composition of a work of art. When engaging with Old Masters, it is not always immediately obvious what we are seeing. All too often the material context in which a work of art originated is unknown, usually time degraded the object, and what we see is obscured by old thick layers of varnish, contamination, wear, and maladroit restoration…

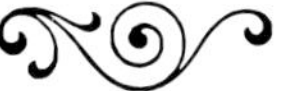

Whenever we are confronted with a work of art previously unknown, we are first and foremost fascinated with what it communicates, what it represents, and for who and by whom it was made. Further we are tempted to discover what can be deduced from the work of art itself. Therefore, we return time and again to the 'art of looking', and as such, we are not that much different from the *amateur curieux* who considered this sport. However, the difference is that aesthetic necessity is less of a concern today than knowledge. And constrained as such, we as connoisseurs started to listen to the artist himself, what he has to say as the art work's creator. During the last decades much has changed in the attitude of art historians who have realized increasingly that material aspects of the work of art have to be taken into consideration. What we are looking at or what we get to see is not always obvious, but when the right tools are utilized in a coherent relationship with historical research, unexpected results often ensue, and sometimes what one would have wished for becomes reality.

The present *Peasants' Dance* is exemplary as a case-study. A long time ago it was discovered by Friedländer, who relying on his legendary trained eye attributed it to Pieter Bruegel the Elder. The work was in such a terrible state of conservation that it never became part of the canonic works of the famous master. However, a recent cleaning and restoration invite us to reassess Friedländer's discovery. We do that with the most recent techniques that we have at our disposal today to complement the thorough traditional art historical analysis. This is the challenge that was taken up by Maximiliaan Martens in this book. The wide range of multidisciplinary approaches that he employs in questioning this work of art is fascinating. He never turns to authoritative statements, but time and again he returns to the nucleus, the very work of art itself. He is aware that the transparency of his argumentation may invite criticism, yet he addresses the reader in all openness. The author is a world-wide acclaimed expert of Flemish painting of the 15th and 16th century. He has written several books and more than a hundred and fifty scholarly articles on major masters such as Jan Van Eyck, Petrus Christus, Hans Memling, Joachim Patinir, Quinten Massys and many others. After his appointment as Associate Professor at the University of Groningen, the Netherlands (1992-2003), he became Full Professor in Art History at Ghent University, Belgium. He is a member of The Royal Flemish Academy of Belgium for Science and the Arts.

It is surprisingly tempting to follow the author in the arguments he provides to re-establish the *Dancing Peasants at a St. Sebastian's Kermis* as an important work by Pieter Bruegel the Elder.

Dr. Paul Huvenne

EMERITUS GENERAL DIRECTOR
ROYAL MUSEUM OF FINE ARTS, ANTWERP.

December 2018

Introduction

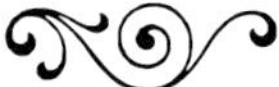

In 2016, we had the good fortune of recognizing under several layers of rather clumsily applied retouching and old overpaint, a painting once attributed to Pieter Bruegel the Elder (?, ca. 1525 – Brussels, 1569) by Max J. Friedländer (Berlin, 1867 – Amsterdam, 1958), the greatest connoisseur of early Flemish painting (Ill. 1). Technical examination and careful cleaning revealed numerous features characteristic of the master's proper style and technique. This variety of evidence compels the reattribution of the painting, representing *Dancing Peasants at a St. Sebastian's Kermis*, back to its original creator and situates it in Pieter Bruegel the Elder's oeuvre (see pp. 18–19). We will simultaneously broaden our scope and discuss the painting's historical place in mid-16th-century Northern European culture.

Pieter Bruegel the Elder, also referred to as 'Pieter Bruegel I', had risen to fame already shortly after his death in 1569. Quite remarkably, at that time most of his works had been acquired by Europe's highest aristocracy and were intensely sought after by notable collectors. Leading Habsburg statesman, Cardinal Granvelle, for instance, was told that they were only available at staggering sums of money. Actually, the lack of available originals by Bruegel created a void in the art market that his eldest son, Pieter II (Brussels, 1564 – Antwerp, 1638) successfully filled by setting up an 'enterprise' of collaborators who produced numerous copies of his father's paintings.[1]

The remarkable fame of the artist contrasts sharply with what we factually know about his life through archival sources, which have been very sparsely preserved. His date and place of birth were already subject to speculation shortly after his death. We do not really know where nor by whom he received his training as a painter, a draughtsman and a designer of prints. Although we have a few indications of the social network in which he took part, his intellectual formation and contacts remain largely obscure. Fortunately, Bruegel's surviving works of art clearly bear witness to his status as a learned and most probably critical man, a so-called *pictor doctus*.

The lack of biographical information is not only frustrating to the 21st-century art historian, but also very remarkable for someone who has been greatly admired almost uninterruptedly since his lifetime to the present day as one of the most prominent artists of Western European art. It challenges us, however, to employ his preserved works as historical sources to the fullest. Fortunately, he signed and dated many of them, which allows us to reconstruct to a large degree his artistic development. Furthermore, his fame among fellow artists is also another important source of information because it left a profound trace of artistic influence. In sum, these are the building blocks at our disposal for reconstructing Bruegel's life and work.

Bruegel's paintings, drawings and prints demonstrate his enormous complexity. His oeuvre originated in one of Europe's most tormented historical periods, an age of religious, social and political conflicts. These circumstances together with the lack of historical certainty about Bruegel's life, gave rise to very divergent views on his work.

Bruegel has been considered as a 'Second Bosch', a humorist with an unusual interest in the excessive behavior of feasting peasants. In the 19th century, he was therefore often referred to as 'the Peasant Bruegel' in order to distinguish him from his sons Pieter II, 'the Hellish', and Jan I, 'the Velvet'. For others he was rather a learned humanist in the wake of Erasmian philosophical thought. As of the 1960s, his presumed position in society shifted from a critic of the Catholic repressive inquisition to an opponent of rising capitalism, while still other authors saw him as a heretic involved in alchemy and occultism. Although the specialized literature on Bruegel brittles with unfounded speculation, the apparent conflicting interpretations are not necessarily mutually exclusive. The complexity of form, content and function are inherent to 16th-century Northern society in general, of which Pieter Bruegel was one of the most brilliant artistic representatives.

During the last decades, experts have made serious attempts to weed out fact from fiction. Paintings and drawings have been withdrawn from the core of Pieter Bruegel the Elder's oeuvre. But fortunately, as new scientific techniques and evidence become available, a precious unknown or completely forgotten artwork resurfaces and a new attribution can be made.

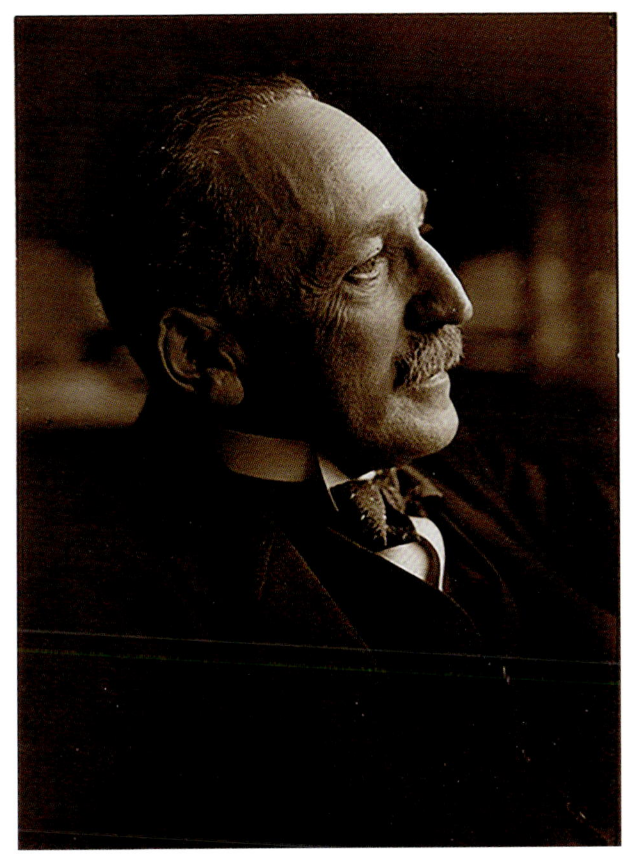

1. MAX J. FRIEDLÄNDER
(Berlin, 1867 – Amsterdam, 1958),
photographer unknown, 1927 © ullstein bild

Prof. dr. Maximiliaan Martens

GHENT UNIVERSITY – ROYAL FLEMISH ACADEMY
OF BELGIUM FOR SCIENCE AND THE ARTS

July 2018

Biography

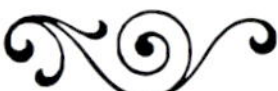

Until 1563, Pieter Bruegel I (ill. 2) worked primarily in Antwerp, one of the largest commercial metropolises in North Western Europe during the early modern times. Like many artists in this booming city, he was an immigrant from elsewhere in the Netherlands attracted by the ample opportunities of finding a suitable clientele. His place of birth is unknown, but as in the case of many immigrants his name has been considered as a toponym, i.e. derived from the place of his origins. Attempts have been made to retrace him to Bruegel, a hammock of what is currently known as Son en Bruegel, a town north of Eindhoven in Northern Brabant (now The Netherlands)(ill. 3). The first great chronicler of Flemish painting, Karel Van Mander (Meulebeke, 1548 – Amsterdam, 1606), situated his birth in Brogel. This might be either Grote Brogel near Maaseik, currently in the Belgian province of Limburg, which in 16th-century sources is often referred to as 'Bruegel', or near 'Kleine Brogel'. Only two years before Bruegel's death, however, the first reference to the painter's birthplace was made by Lodovico Guicciardini (Florence, 1521 – Antwerp, 1589), a Florentine merchant residing in Antwerp. In his descriptive account of the Low Countries, *Descrittione di tutti I Paesi Bassi* (1567), Guicciardini situated the artist's birthplace in Breda, one of the major towns of Brabant, about 50 km NNE of Antwerp. Contrary to these smaller villages, Breda was an artistic hub at the time, where Pieter's contemporary, the portrait painter Willem Key (Breda, ca. 1515 – Antwerp, 1568), also originated from. Hitherto, this biographic issue still remains unsolved.

It remains equally unclear when Pieter was born and direct information on his education and early career is scarce. He became a free master in the Antwerp painters' guild of Saint Luc in 1551. Statistical research has shown that people attained this status often at the age of maturity, which was 25 years old at the time. If this were also the case for Bruegel, he may have been born around 1526. He was recorded for the first time in the written

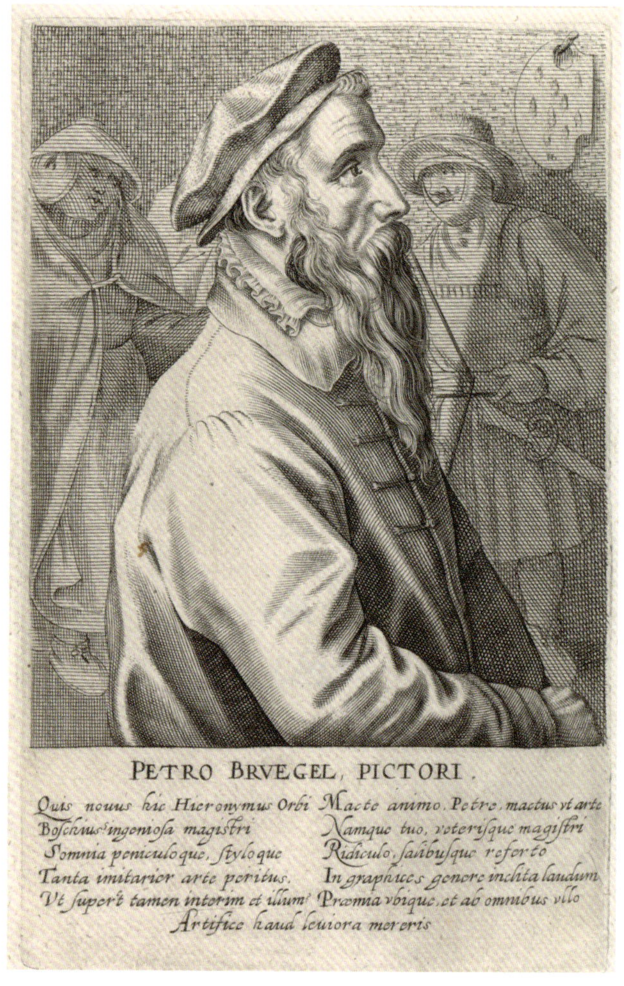

2. JOHANNES WIERIX,
PORTRAIT OF PIETER BRUEGEL THE ELDER
engraving, in Dominicus Lampsonius, *Pictorum aliquot celebrium Germaniae inferioris effigies*, ed. Volcxken Diericx, Antwerp 1572, plate 19
© UGent, Universiteitsbibliotheek

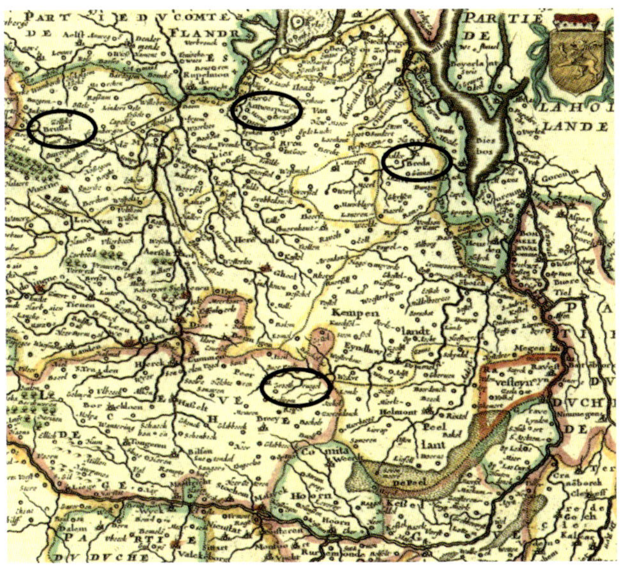

3. Map of Brabant indicating Bruegel's possible birthplaces and places of activity, Groningen University © Groningen University

sources in 1550-1551, when he acted as a workshop assistant to his almost exact contemporary, Pieter Balten (Antwerp, 1525–1584) on an altarpiece for the glove makers' guild in Mechelen. Van Mander, in turn, informs us that Bruegel was an apprentice in the workshop of the prominent painter-designer Pieter Coecke van Aelst (Aalst, 1502 – Brussels, 1550). Apart from being Bruegel's teacher, Pieter Coecke also became his father-in-law, when Pieter married his daughter Mayken in 1563. This life event may explain why he acquired free mastership immediately after Coecke as head of the workshop had died. After all, it was not unusual that collaborators became independent after their master died and even took over the business. Pieter Coecke himself had made the same move in 1527, when his master and father-in-law, Jan Mertens van Dornicke (Tournai, c. 1470 – Antwerp, 1527) deceased. Remarkably, Pieter Bruegel's earliest work resembles by no means the style of his presumed master, Pieter Coecke. One might interpret that as Bruegel developed his own manner very early on in his career, or that Coecke's style had become outdated by 1550.

While we are kept in the dark about most of Pieter Bruegel the Elder's early career, we do have more information as of 1552, when, just after having become an independent master, he ventured on a long journey of nearly two years to Italy. A recent study based on his signed drawings reconstructed his trip via the

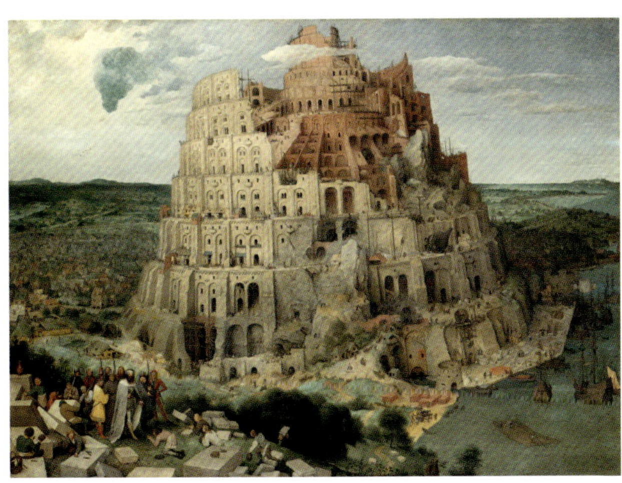

4. PIETER BRUEGEL THE ELDER, *THE TOWER OF BABEL*, 1563
oil on panel, Vienna, Kunsthistorisches Museum
© Vienna, Kunsthistorisches Museum

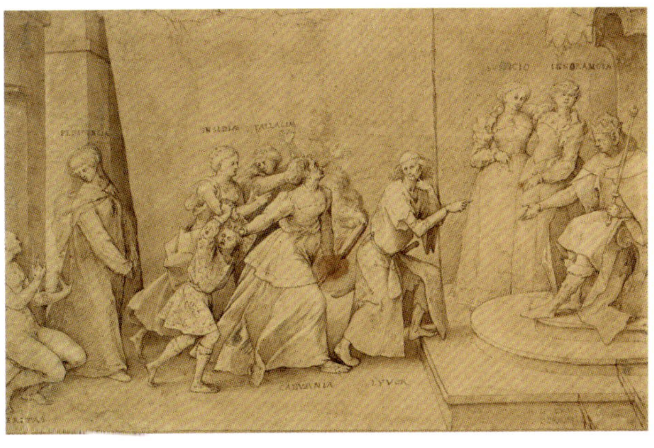

5. PIETER BRUEGEL THE ELDER, *CALUMNY OF APELLES*
pen and brown ink with brown wash on brown paper, London, British Museum
© BMimages

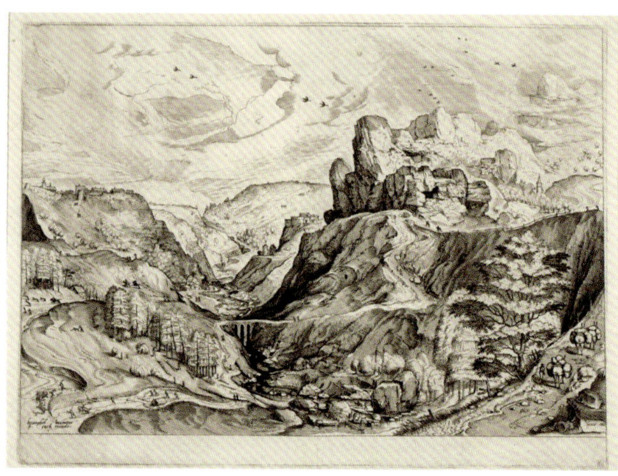

6. *ALPINE LANDSCAPE*
engraving by Joannes en Lucas Doetecum after a drawing by Pieter Brugel the Elder, published by Hieronymus Cock, c. 1555-56 © BMimages

Provence, the Mediterranean coast, to Rome, continuing south as far as Sicily, and returning over the Alps.[2] Bruegel's response to antique culture remained rather restricted, be it that his two versions of the *Tower of Babel*, (Rotterdam, Museum Boijmans-Van Beuningen and Vienna, Kunsthistorisches Museum, ill. 4), are clearly inspired by the Roman Coliseum. His interest in more recent Italian art seems to have been equally luke-warm, although his drawing, *Calumny of Apelles* (London, British Museum, ill. 5) is unthinkable without Botticelli's example.

On the other hand, the sublime majesty of the Alps made a profound impression on our artist. Van Mander eloquently described this impression as if "*he had swallowed those mountains and rocks, and back home spit them back on his canvasses and panels.*"[3] Hieronymus Cock (Antwerp, 1518–1570) published some of these drawings as prints in his publishing house 'Aux Quatre Vents' (ill. 6). After his return from Italy in 1553, Bruegel continued designing prints for Cock. It even seems that this was his major occupation until around 1557, when his first dated paintings originated. Van Mander also disclosed information about Bruegel's personality by describing the artist as a quiet, but jolly man, who became inspired by Bosch, which left him with the nick-name 'Pier den Drol' (Pieter the Turd). His works triggered a smile on the faces of their observers. With a very close friend, the merchant Hans Franckert, he enjoyed attending peasants' kermises and weddings, where equally dressed like the peasants themselves, they had fun with their customs and demeanor.

After his marriage to Mayken Coecke in 1563, the young couple moved to Brussels. It is again Van Mander who provided more details about this event. It would have been his mother-in-law, Mayken Verhulst, Pieter Coecke's widow, who insisted on this move, as she wanted to prevent Pieter from maintaining contact with another woman.

Only six years later, on 9 September 1569, Pieter Bruegel I died and was interred in the Chapel Church, in the center of Brussels (ill. 7). Van Mander knew that on his deathbed, Pieter asked his wife to destroy some of his drawings as to avoid that she would run into

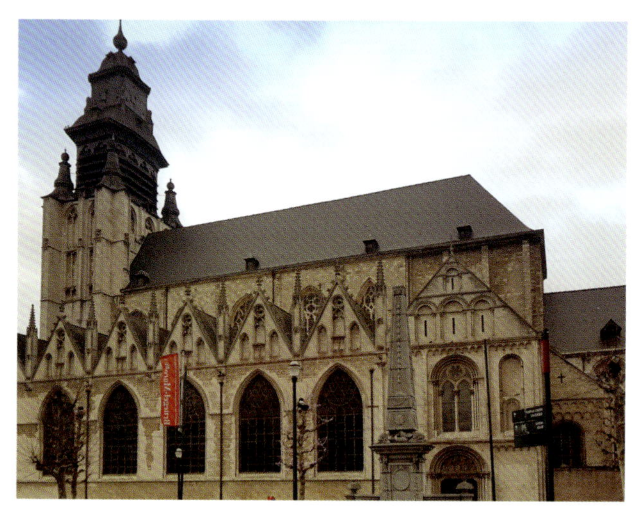

7. Brussels, Chapel Church

problems. It is especially this request that engendered speculation about Bruegel's controversial political points of view. He left his widow with two little children, Pieter II (Brussels, 1564 – Antwerp, 1638) and Jan I (Brussels, 1568 – Antwerp, 1625), who, according to Van Mander, were trained as painters by their grandmother, Mayken Verhulst. This younger generation wrote their name as 'Brueghel' (with 'h'), an orthography that Pieter I himself had consequently changed to Bruegel (without 'h') as of 1559. As already mentioned, Pieter Brueghel II, continued to promote his father's original works by producing large numbers of copies. Jan Brueghel I, however, much more talented than his older brother, became an original artist who was highly praised and collaborated with renowned contemporaries such as Pieter Paul Rubens.

Only three years after Bruegel's death, Domenicus Lampsonius (Bruges, c. 1536 – Liège, 1599) included the artist in his *Pictorum aliquot celebrium Germaniae inferioris effigie* (1572)(ill. 2), a eulogy of 23 famous Netherlandish artists with etched portraits, among whom, evidently, Pieter Bruegel the Elder is included. First praised as a 'new Bosch', Lampsonius changed his appreciation in the second edition (ed. 1600) by stating that Bruegel was the most important artist of his time. It is not known whether Lampsonius ever met Pieter Bruegel in person. The prominent cartographer, geographer and humanist, Abraham Ortelius (Antwerp, 1527–1598), however, was a

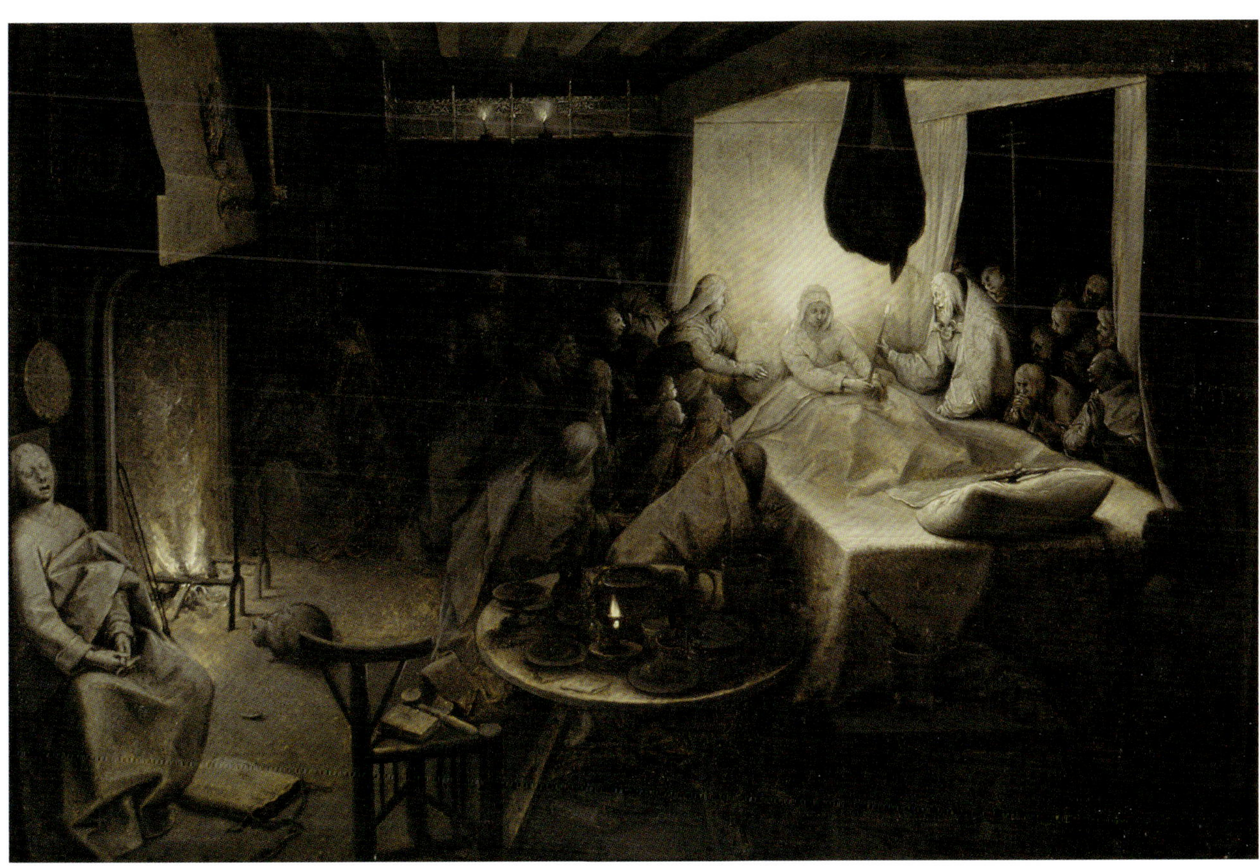

8. PIETER BRUEGEL THE ELDER, *DEATH OF THE VIRGIN*
in grisaille, oil on panel, Banbury, Upton House, National Trust
© National Trust Images

personal friend of the artist and even owned a work by him, the *Death of the Virgin* in grisaille (now Banbury, Upton House, National Trust, ill. 8). In addition to being famous as the publisher of the *Theatrum Orbis Terrarum* (1570), the first modern atlas, Ortelius wrote an *Album Amicorum* in 1573, in which he mourned his talented friend's early death. Just as Lampsonius, Oretlius called Bruegel "*doubtlessly, the most important painter of his time*" and praised the naturalist representation of his subjects. Nature was his sole model, he even "*painted many things which cannot be painted, offering more to think about than can be observed*". Also Karel Van Mander, our most informative (but not always trustworthy) source for Bruegel's life, praised the master's imitation of nature in his *Schilder-boeck* (1604), a skill that he picked up especially during his journey to Italy.

Possibly, Bruegel had also opponents who claimed that his art does not really conform to the Flemish artistic tradition nor to the idealized 'Romanist' art of his contemporaries. The Ghent rethoritician, Lucas d'Heere (Ghent, 1534 – ?, 1584), was not only one of the most avid admirers of Jan van Eyck, but also of his own teacher Frans Floris (Antwerp 1519/20–1570), without doubt Bruegel's absolute artistic counterpart among mid-16th century Antwerp painters. In a particular passage in one of his most famous writings, *Den Hof ende Boomgaerd der Poesien* (The Garden and Orchard of Poetry, 1565), he fulminates on a certain '*Quidam, painter who insulted the painters of Antwerp*'. Quidam had been in Rome, but no trace of antiquity nor contemporary great Italian masters was found in his work that was painted "*more bitter than gall*" in the inferior technique of canvas painting. According to a number of experts, this 'Quidam' is no one else other than Pieter Bruegel, who indeed often painted on canvas. Possibly d'Heere's text reflects an art theoretical debate that opposed the rather traditional, slickly painted, elevated 'Romanist' art of Floris, to the avant-gardist, rough and simple execution of peasant scenes by Pieter Bruegel I. Floris' art consists of allegories invoking knowledge about classical antiquity, whereas Bruegels' paintings are more direct critical and moralistic allegories of contemporary life. However, there can be little doubt that both primarily addressed the social urban elite.

A Rediscovered Painting

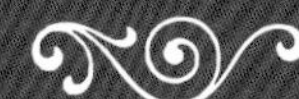

PIETER BRUEGEL THE ELDER
DANCING PEASANTS
AT A ST. SEBASTIAN'S KERMIS
oil on panel, private collection © UGent, Gicas, 2018

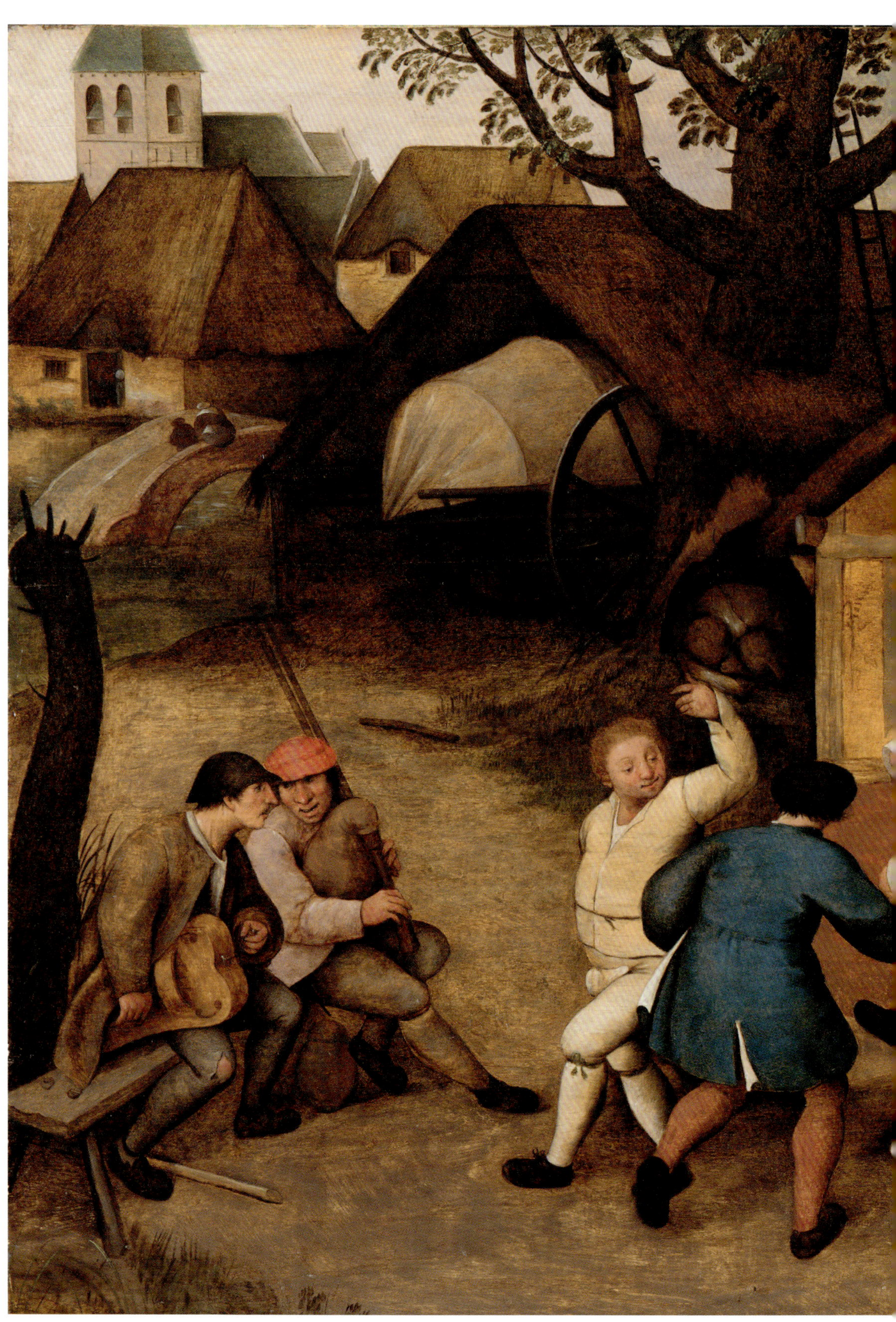

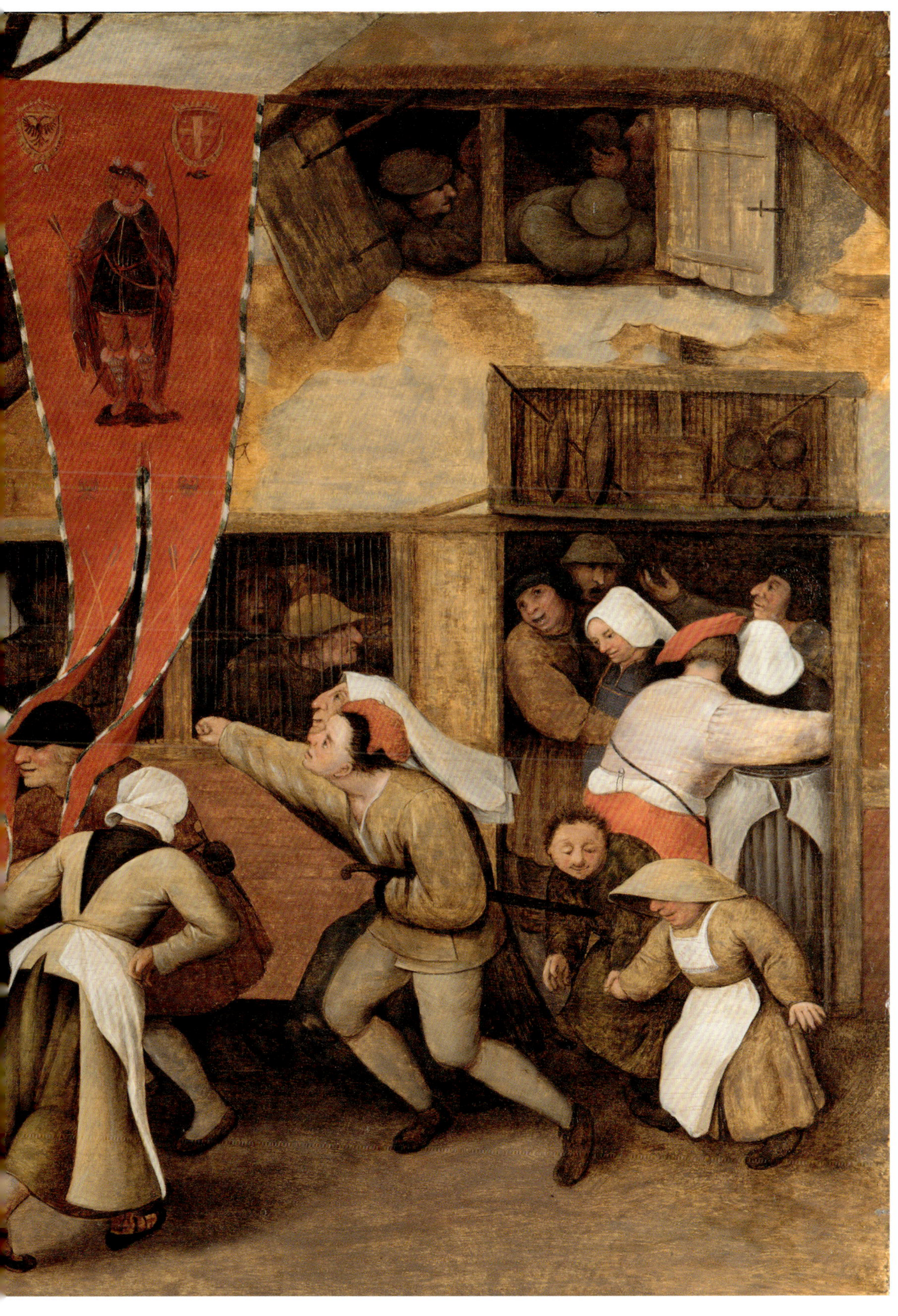

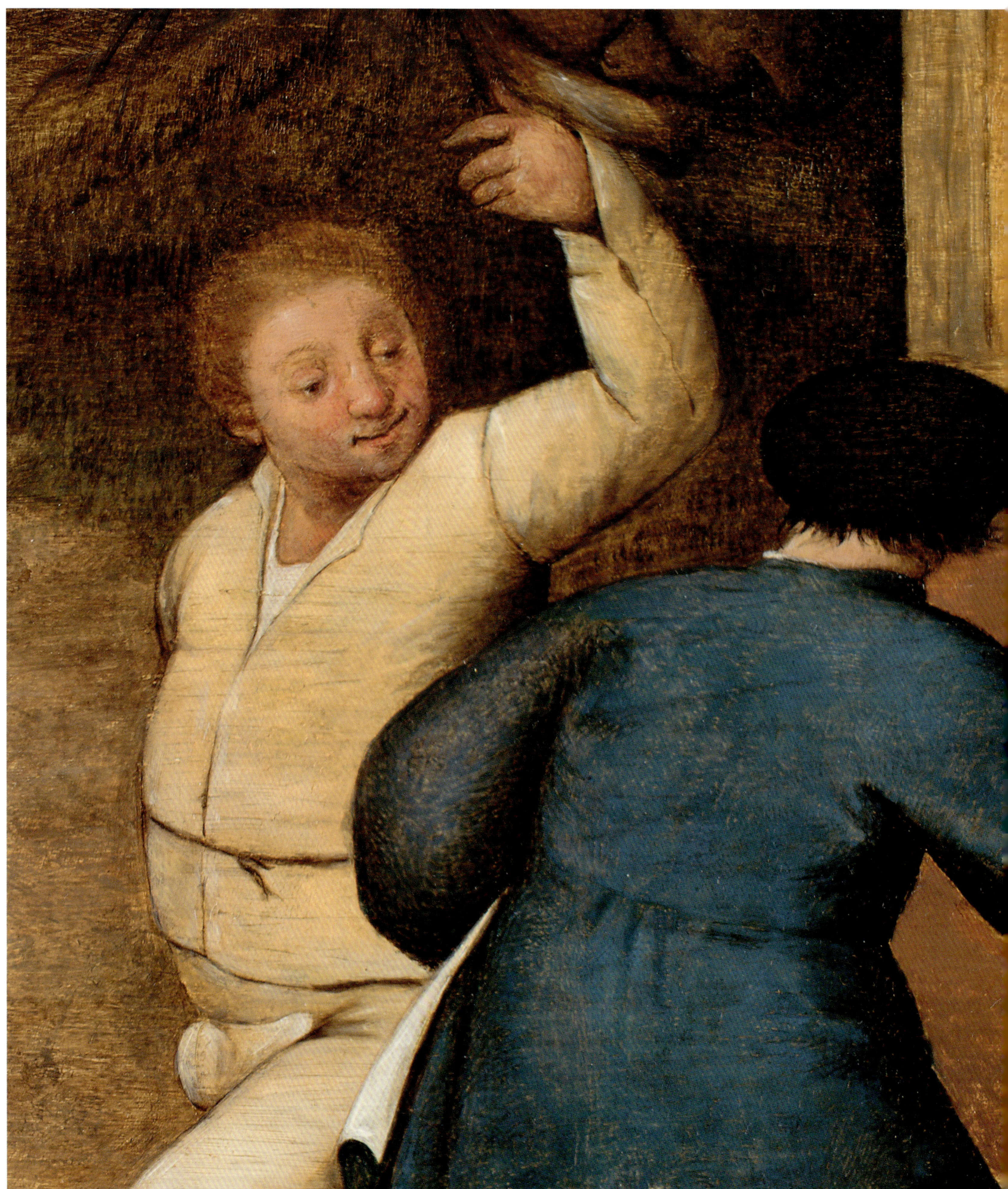

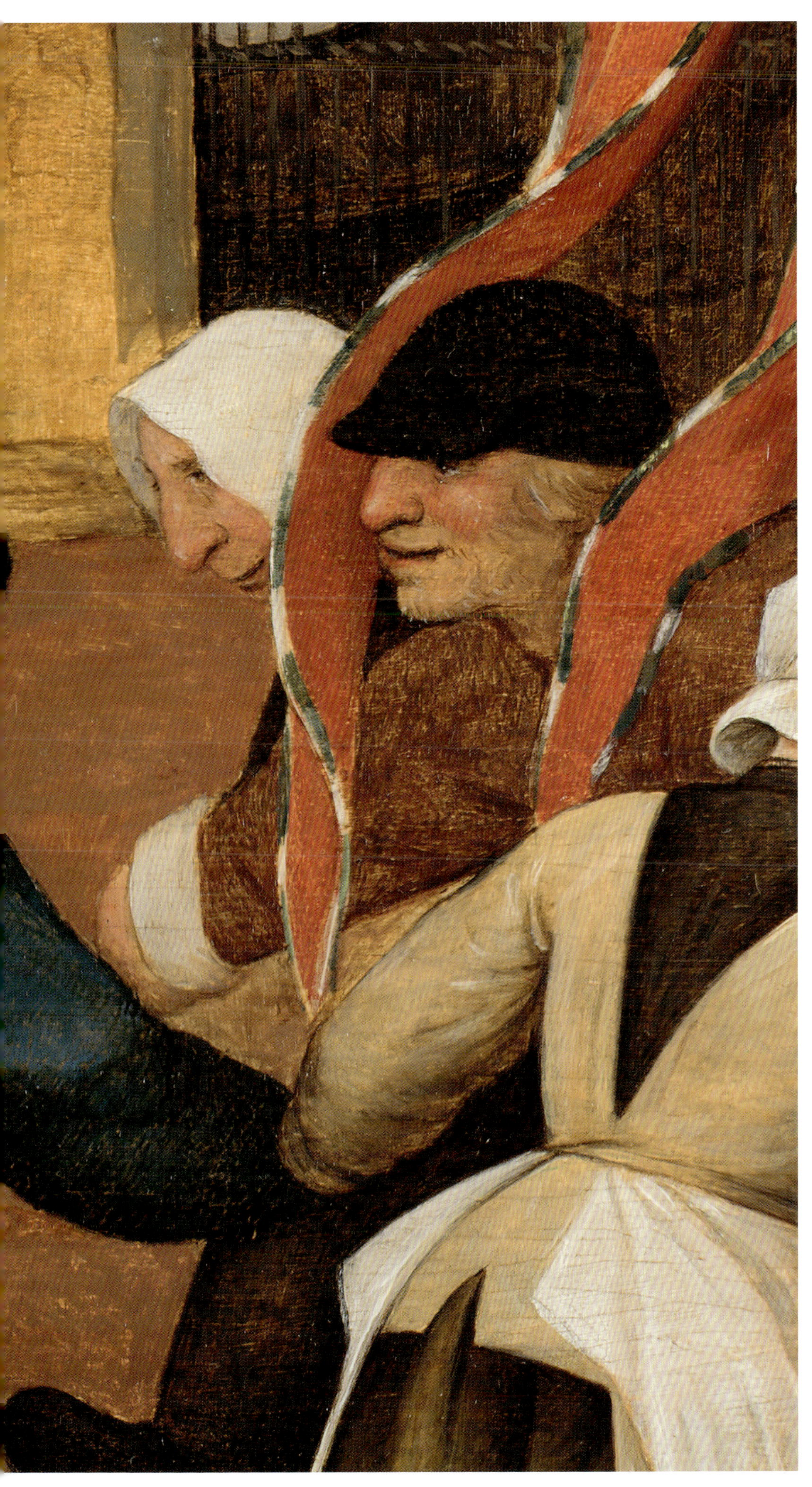

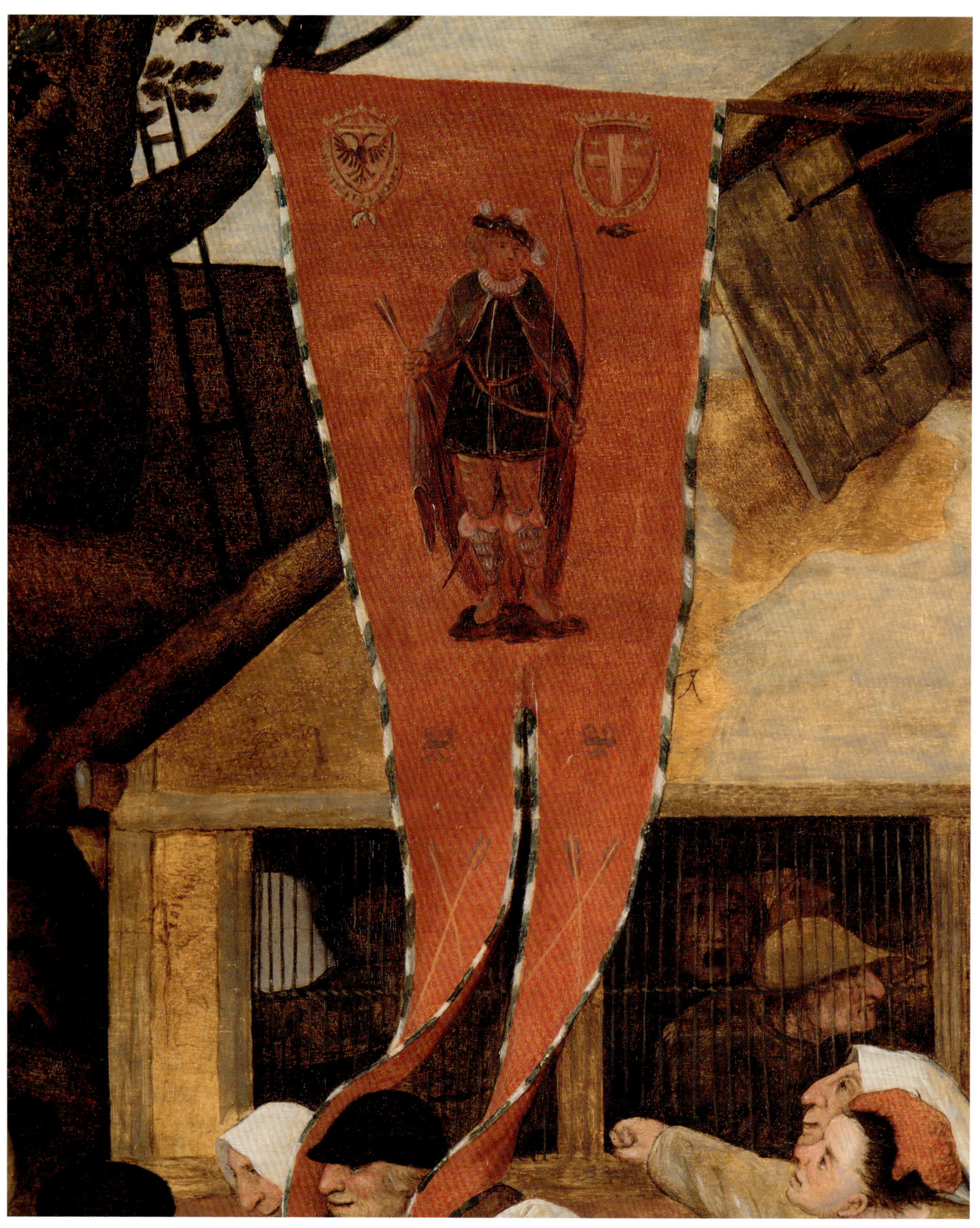

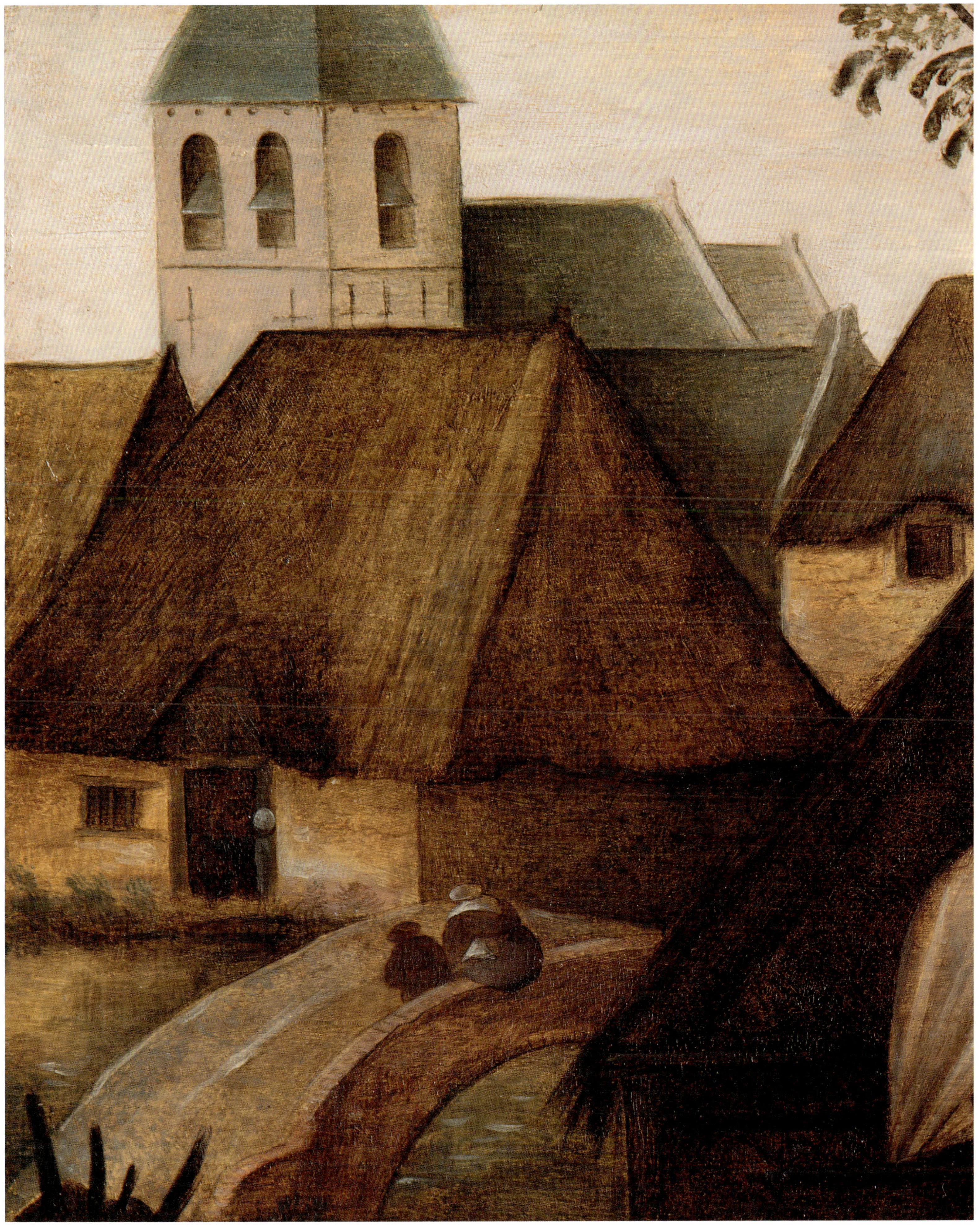

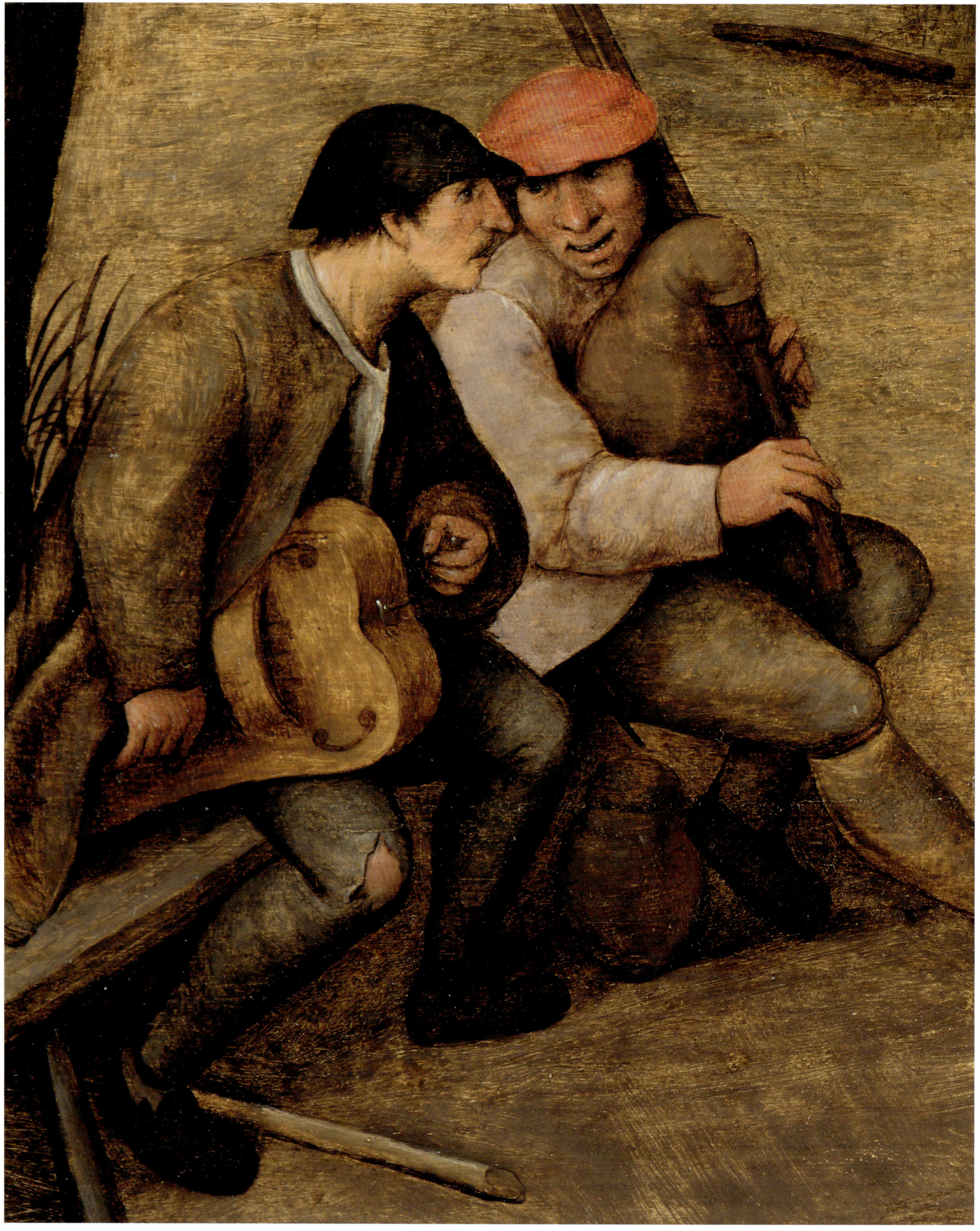

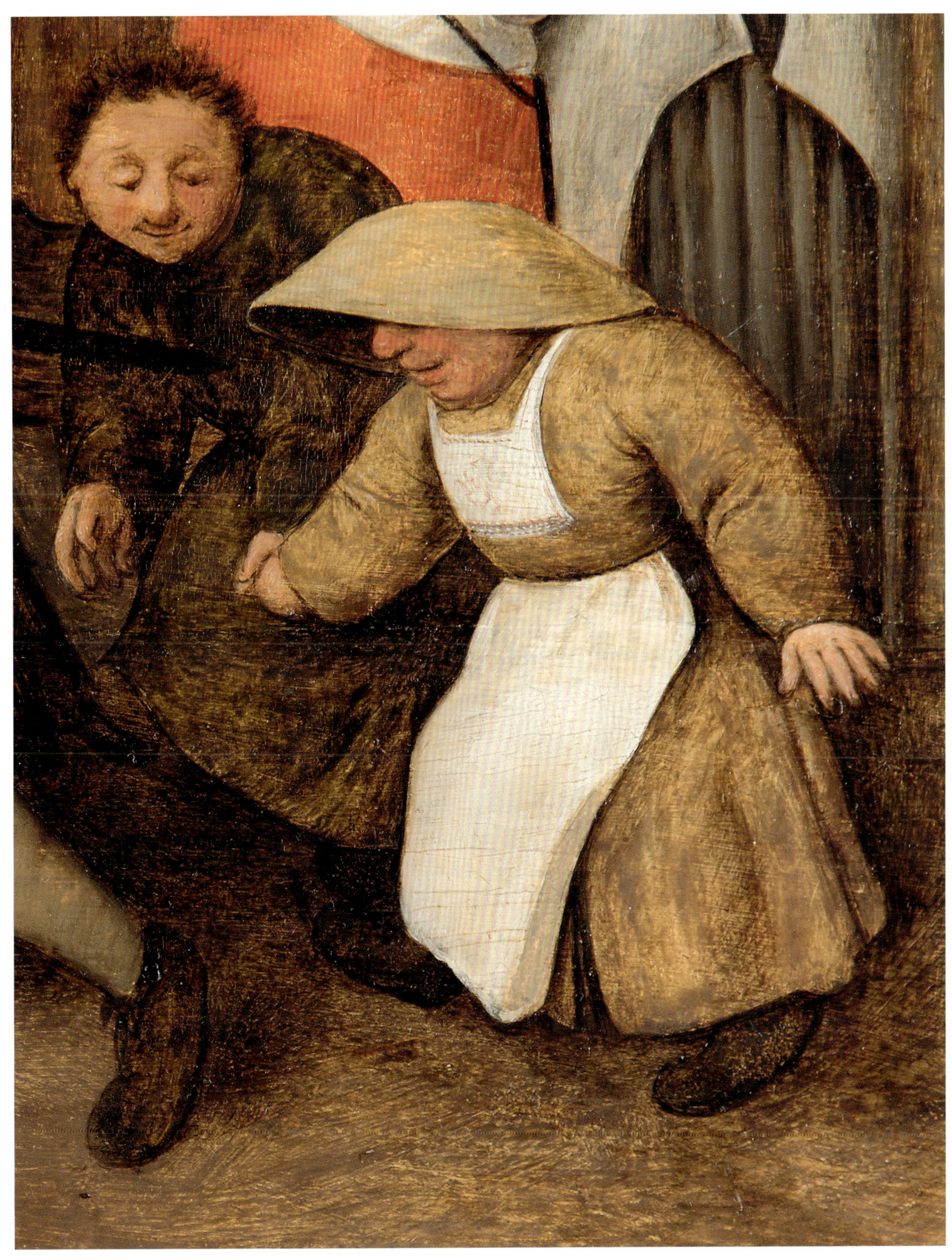

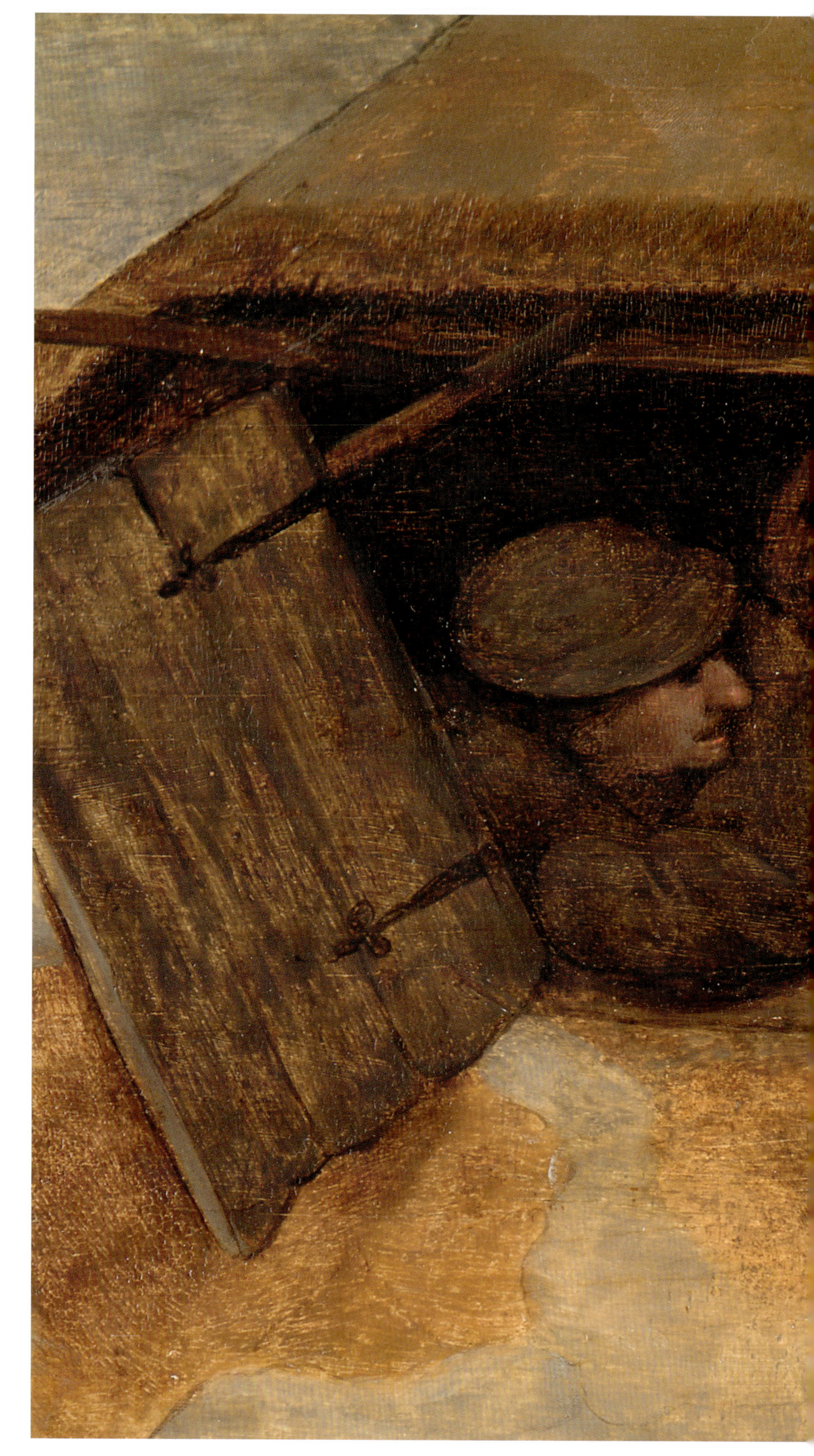

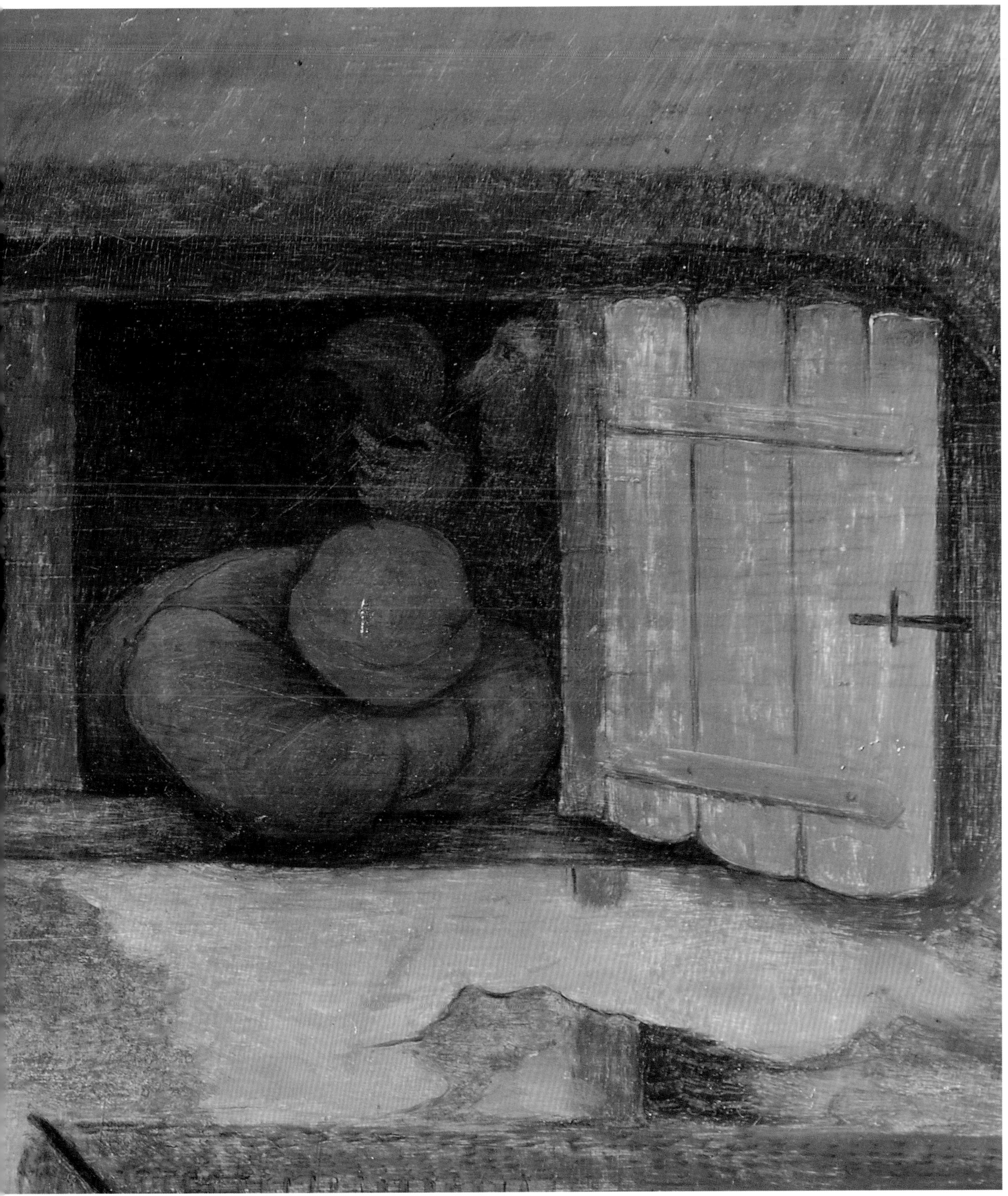

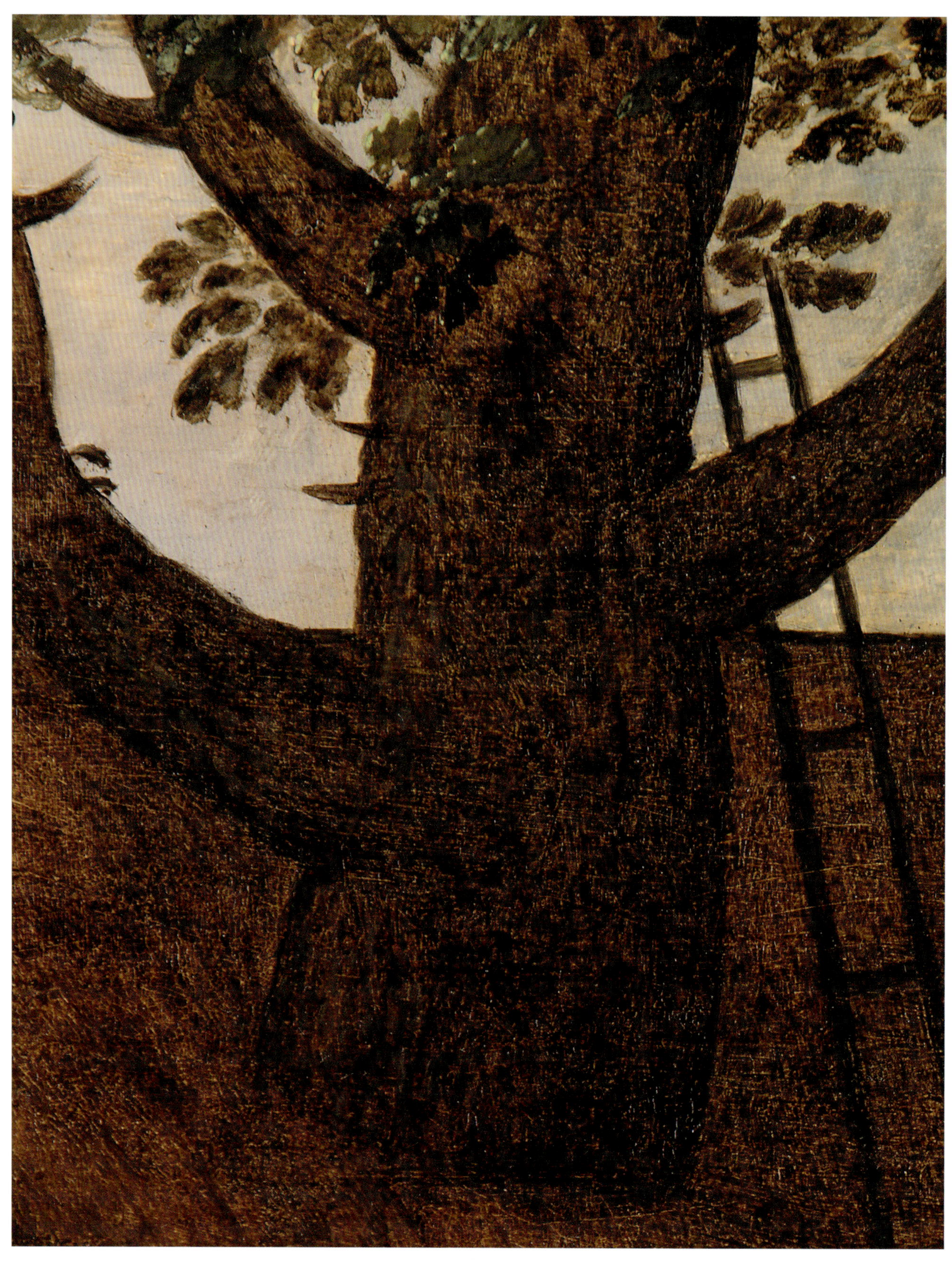

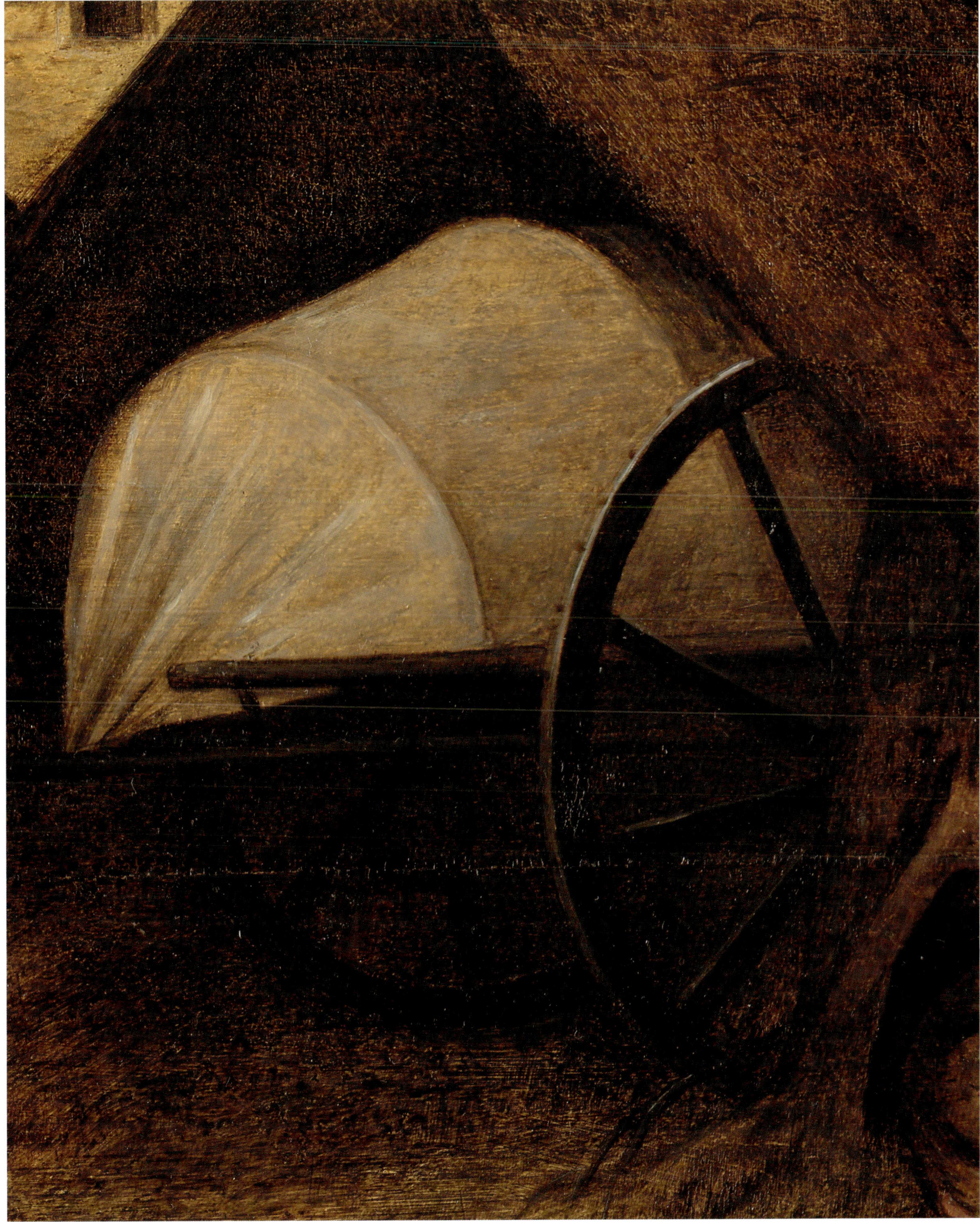

Iconography: Peasants' Kermises in Bruegel's Oeuvre

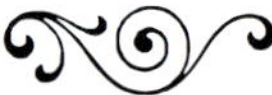

A rather corpulent young man, followed by three couples and two children, is dancing as he leaves a very crowded country inn, adorned with a large banner (see pp. 18–19). Two musicians, a bagpiper and one who plays the hurdy-gurdy, are talking to each other in the left foreground. Two loving couples stand in the doorway of the inn. Through the window one observes on-looking people, gesticulating and yelling. Upstairs, more people can be seen, one drinking, another one, probably already drunk, hangs sleeping out of the window. To the left side of the inn a large dog is sleeping in the shade of a shelter. The architectural construction that accommodates the crowd can be identified as an inn by the depiction of breads above the entrance and the large banner hanging from a pole.

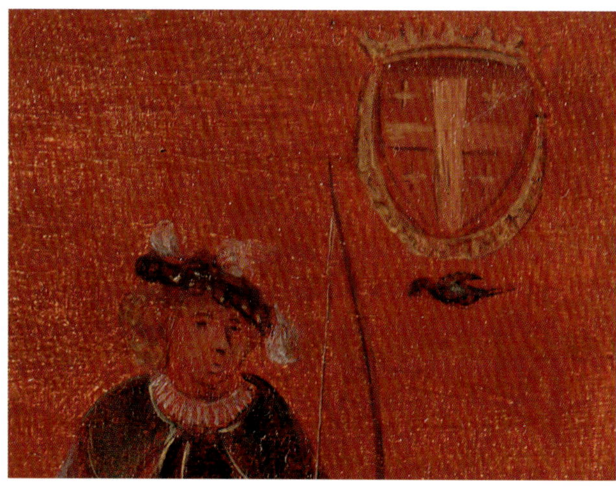

9. Coat of arms of the St. Sebastian's guild
Det. of ill. pp. 18 –19 © UGent, Gicas, 2018

Not everyone has gathered in the village's inn. A couple, possibly a mother and a son, is resting on the bridge in the left background. A woman stands in the doorway of a house close by. Behind that in the far background, other houses surround the village's church. In a stable a large chariot is stalled.

From a window of the inn, the villagers have hung up a large red split banner, rimmed with an alternating black and white boarder. It bears the representation of a richly dressed bowman. He is either a generic member of the bowmen's guild, or its patron saint, St. Sebastian. The latter identification is less likely as the saint is usually shown half-naked pierced by several arrows.[4] Be that as it may, the connection to the bowmen's guild of St. Sebastian cannot be denied. The coat of arms of that guild figures on the heraldic upper left of the banner (*in gueulles, a cross of or, accompanied by four crosses of the same*) (ill. 9). The black bird hanging from the collar around the coat of arms represents the bowmen's shooting target. These guilds stood under the protection of the sovereign, which is exemplified by the crown and the Burgundian collar itself and, to the heraldic right, by the imperial coat of arms of the Holy Roman Empire (*in or, a double headed eagle of sable*), surrounded by the chain of the Order of the Golden Fleece.

In other words, the banner of the St. Sebastian's guild clarifies the scene depicted in the painting: it is a kermis somewhere in Brabant dedicated to St. Sebastian or organized by the bowmen's guild of the locality.

Far better known examples of peasant representations in Bruegel's oeuvre are the famous *Wedding Dance* (Detroit, Institute of Arts) (ill. 10), the *Peasants' Wedding* (ill. 11), and *Peasants' Kermis* (both Vienna, Kunsthistorisches Museum) (ill. 12). Those works are larger in size, represent far more figures and are thus more complex compositions than the *Dancing*

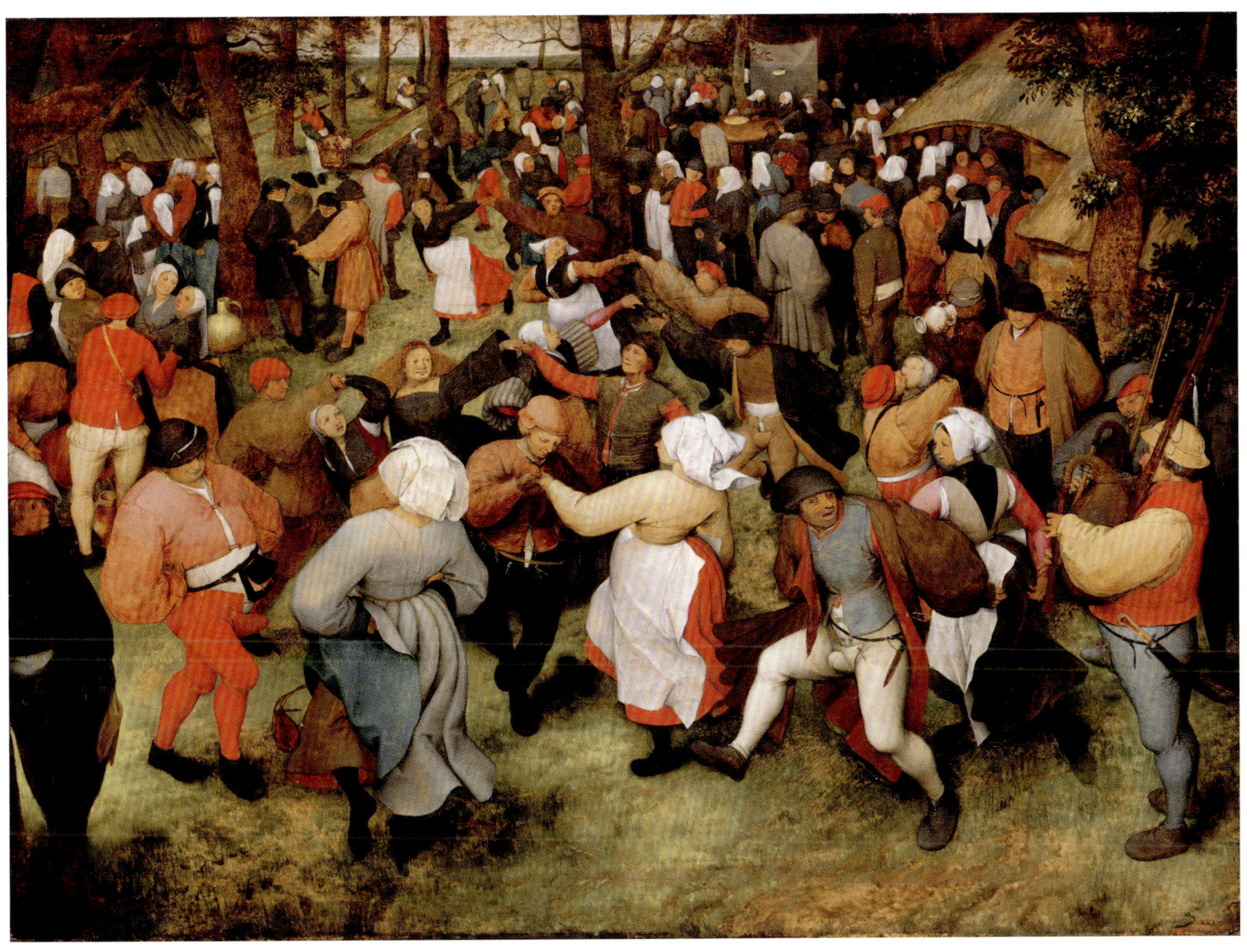

10. PIETER BRUEGEL THE ELDER, *WEDDING DANCE*
c. 1566, oil on panel, Detroit, Detroit Institute of Arts © Bridgeman Images

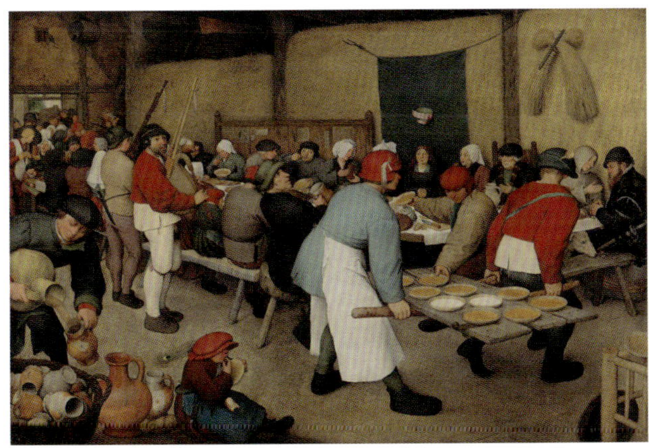

11. PIETER BRUEGEL THE ELDER,
PEASANTS' WEDDING
c. 1567, oil on panel, Vienna, Kunsthistorisches Museum
© Vienna, Kunsthistorisches Museum

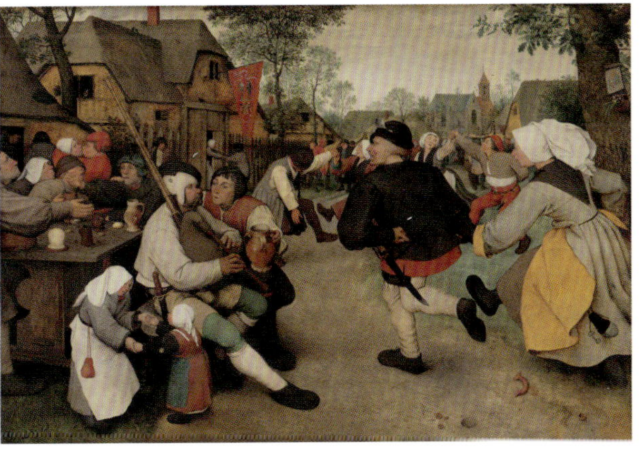

12. PIETER BRUEGEL THE ELDER,
PEASANTS' KERMIS
c. 1567, oil on panel, Vienna, Kunsthistorisches Museum
© Vienna, Kunsthistorisches Museum

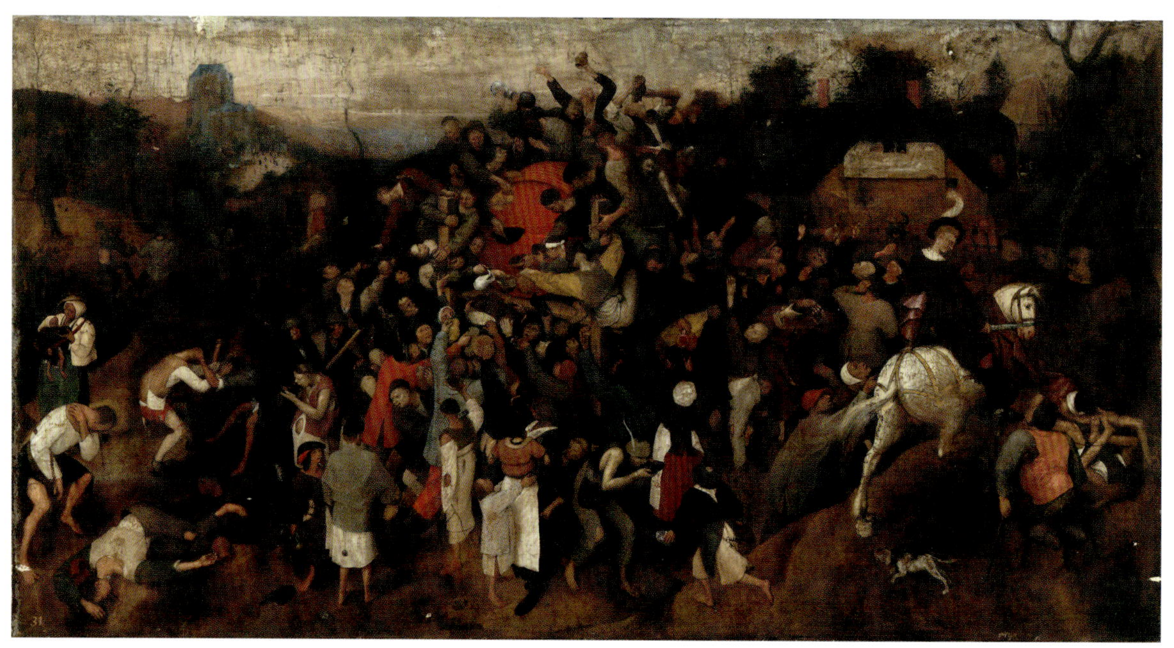

13. PIETER BRUEGEL THE ELDER,
WINE OF ST. MARTIN'S DAY
tempera on canvas, Madrid, Museo del Prado © Museo del Prado Madrid

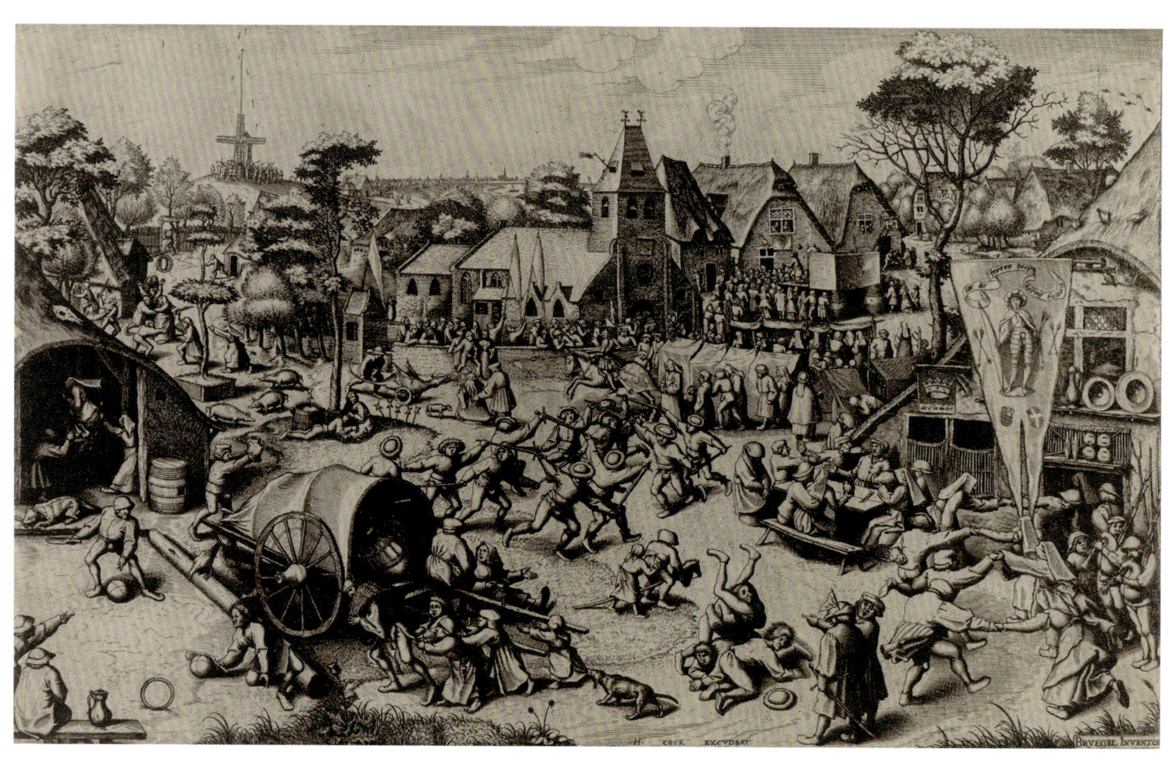

14. *KERMIS OF ST. GEORGES*
engraving published by Hieronymus Cock after a lost drawing by Pieter Bruegel I
© BMimages

Peasants at a St. Sebastian's Kermis. However, as we will see, their moralistic meaning is very similar.

Another example of a village kermis in Bruegel's preserved oeuvre is the recently discovered *Wine of St. Martin's Day* (Madrid, Museo del Prado)(ill. 13),[5] which celebrates the new wine made of the recent harvest of grapes on 11 November, St. Martin's Eve. Here, this complex multi-figured composition morally opposes the generosity of Saint Martin dividing his cloak with a beggar and the gluttony and selfishness of the drunken crowd indulging in the free wine.

The actual historical meaning of the *Dancing Peasants at a St. Sebastian's Kermis* is revealed by its drawn and engraved counter pieces, such as the *Kermis of St. Georges*, published by Hieronymus Cock after a lost drawing by Pieter Bruegel I, as exemplified by the inscription 'BRUEGEL INVENTOR' (ill. 14).[6] St. Georges is the patron of the crossbow shooters' guilds, which existed (and often still exist) alongside the guild of St. Sebastian in towns across the Low Countries. As in the *St. Sebastian's Kermis*, a similar banner with the patron saint is hanging from an inn at the right-hand side of this print. Besides his representation and coats-of-arms, the banner also carries an inscription: '*Laet die boeren haer kermis houuen*' (Let the peasants keep their kermis). It is telling that in the right foreground, two men, one of whom is pointing to the feasting people in the scene, are talking to one another. In the lower left corner another man equally points out the display of folly to his son, a motif known from the famous Bruegel drawing of 1556 *Big Fishes Eating the Small Ones* (Vienna, Albertina).

Compositionally, *Dancing Peasants at a St. Sebastian's Kermis* is closely related to the left side of Bruegel's drawing *Kermis at Hoboken*

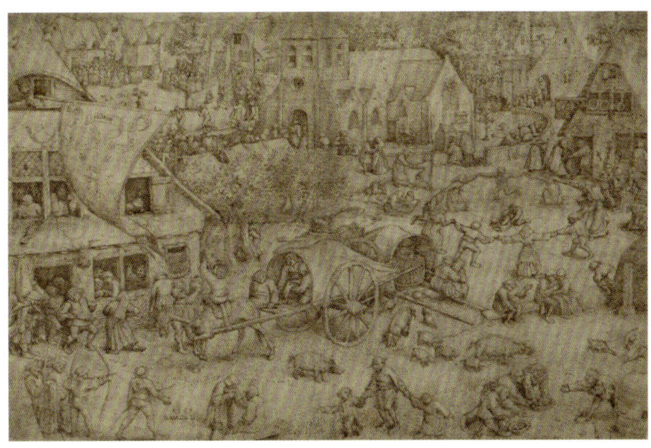

15. PIETER BRUEGEL THE ELDER, *KERMIS AT HOBOKEN*
1559, pen and brown ink, Samuel Courtauld Trust: Lee Bequest, 1947
© The Courtauld Gallery

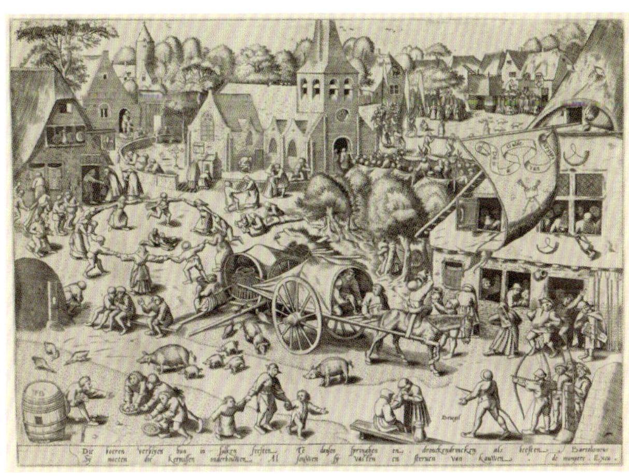

16. *KERMIS AT HOBOKEN*,
after 1559, engraving by Frans Hogenberg, published by Bartholomeus de Momper after a drawing by Pieter Bruegel I © Amsterdam, Rijksmuseum

(London, Courtauld Institute) and (evidently in reverse) Pieter Hogenberg's print made after it (ill. 15–16). Dancing peasants equally leave a crowded inn from which hangs the banner of a shooting guild.

Both Catholics and Protestants alike fiercely criticized village kermises on feast days of saints. The Council of Trent explicitly condemned excess and drunkenness on holy days as abusive conduct.[7] Also the reformed

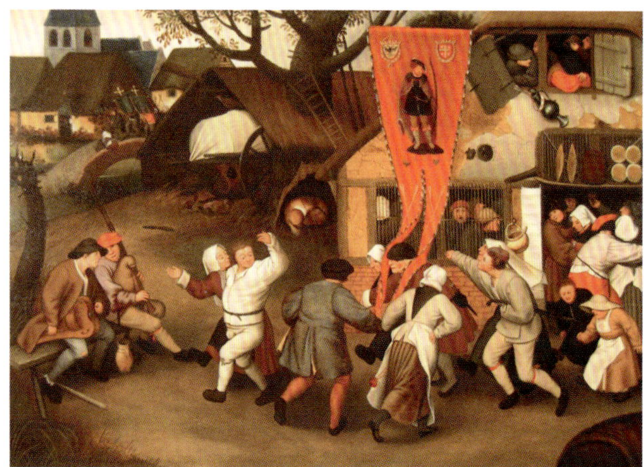

17. Copy attributed to MARTEN VAN CLEVE I (Antwerp, 1527–1581) oil on panel, Belgium, private collection © UGent, Gicas, 2018

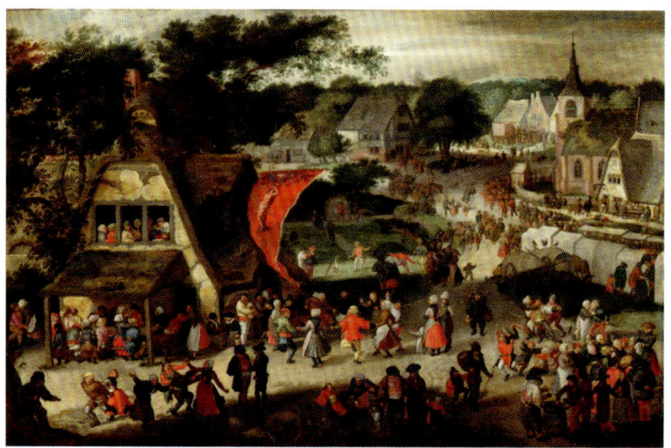

18. JACOB SAVERY, *ST. SEBASTIAN'S KERMIS* c. 1598, oil on panel, The Hague, Mauritshuis © Mauritshuis The Hague

teacher Petrus Bloccius rallied against 'so-called holy days' that were not much more than occasions at which inns were filled with drunks doing nothing.[8] In 1559, King Philip II decreed even that the Hoboken kermis had to be restricted to one day instead of the usual three. Of course, this decree dismayed the Antwerp citizens for whom it was a popular destination as taxes on beer were lower there than in the city, which made it much cheaper.[9] This event made the representation of peasant kermises, and especially that of Hoboken, popular in the repertoire of Bruegel and his followers.[10]

The inscription underneath Hogenberg's print of Hoboken Kermis provides further evidence for the iconographical meaning of such depictions: '*Die boeren verblijen hun in sulken feesten Te dansen springhen en dronckendrincken als beesten. / Sij moeten die kermissen onderhouwen Al souwen sij vasten en sterven van kauwen*' (The peasants are having fun at such feasts: dancing, jumping and excessive drinking like beasts. They will maintain such kermises even if they have to fast and die of cold).

These moralizing inscriptions on prints, passive onlookers and pointing commentators have been related to Van Mander's account mentioned earlier that Pieter Bruegel enjoyed attending peasant parties in the countryside in the company of his friend, Hans Franckert. Together they would dress up as peasants themselves, offer gifts and pretend they were relatives of the groom or bride.

> "*Here, Bruegel entertained himself observing the nature of the peasants in eating, drinking, dancing, leaping, lovemaking and other amusements, which he then most animatedly and subtly imitated with paint, in watercolor as well as oil paints, for he was most outstanding in the handling of both techniques...*"[11]

Traditionally, this has been interpreted as the condescending attitude of the urban elite towards people from the countryside. However, in the early 16th century, Erasmus still testified to a positive attitude towards peasants:

> "*If you look for manners of everyday life, there is no race more open to humanity and kindness, or less given to wildness or ferocious behavior. It is a straightforward nature, without treachery or deceit, and not prone to any serious vices, (so much) to pleasure, especially of feasting.*"[12]

In a few decades, not so much the attitude towards people living outside the cities had changed, but also, as recent scholarship has shown, the religiously inspired ethics concerning excessive behavior of both country and city folks alike.[13] In the opposition between Roman Catholics and Calvinists in general, the role of sin and good deeds became a crucial issue in the debate pro and contra predestination. This explains the prominence of the representation of the Capital Sins and the Virtues in the oeuvre of Pieter Bruegel the Elder. Moreover, also working ethics and views on social politics, like dealing with poverty, were rapidly changing among the elite in the expanding metropolis.

It remains very difficult to pinpoint with precision Bruegel's personal point of view on the matter. Wasn't he more a silent, ironic and witty observer of his time than a fierce moralist? A humanist, too critical to choose blindly sides in the political, social and religious conflicts of his time?

A rather faithful copy attributed to Marten van Cleve I (Antwerp, 1527–1581) is known of our painting (private collection, Belgium) (ill. 17).[14] Small additions to the composition are noteworthy: the dancer in front is accompanied by a rather clumsily painted woman and in the right foreground lays a large wine barrel. The building is more clearly identifiable as an inn by a pitcher hanging from the window. The figures on the bridge are watching an approaching procession. These clarifications are needed in more complex compositions, but here they take away some of the typical subtle Bruegelian image puzzle, his way of having the observer gradually discovering the image's meaning.[15] By adding a procession in the background, it becomes obviously clear that the people on the bridge turn themselves to the devotional practice on the saint's feast day and away from the jolly party on the foreground that doubtlessly will end up in excessive alcohol abuse and lascivious behavior. The most striking difference between this copy and its original is the stiffness in the figures' movements.

Other (partial) copies of *Dancing Peasants at a St. Sebastian's Kermis* survive in the large oeuvre attributed to Pieter Brueghel II and his circle; yet, often only the inn and the banner with the saint were copied.[16] Next generations of Bruegel followers adapted the subject of the Village Kermis of St. Sebastian, but like that of St. Georges often seen from a point of view further away and with innumerable figures. A known example is Jacob Savery's version at the Mauritshuis in The Hague (ill. 18), where the saint on the banner appears more traditionally as a half-naked man pierced with arrows.[17] David Vinckboons (Mechelen, 1576 – Amsterdam, 1631/33), in turn, relocated the St. Sebastian's Kermis from a village to the setting of the town of Oudenaarde in Flanders in a drawing from 1602 (Copenhagen, SMK, The Royal Collection of Graphic Art).[18] In such compositional approaches, the original meaning of Pieter Bruegel the Elder's original painting was diluted. Bruegel's subtle morality had made place for pure visual sensation.

Materials and Condition

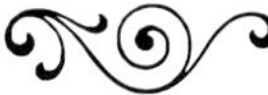

In current art historical research increasingly more attention is devoted to the materials used and the artistic or artisanal techniques that were employed to create an art object. The type of materials and the way they were crafted provides important information on the place and time where an object has been produced. Sometimes, it is even typical for a particular artist, in which case it can be used as a determining factor in attribution, expanding objectively traditional connoisseurship, which is based exclusively on visual observations and stylistic analysis. Also the state of preservation or condition of the object is studied to determine the degree in which it has survived in its original state.

The identification of painting materials is usually done through chemical analysis, although microscopic analysis under great magnification may provide valuable clues. The study of historical practical handbooks combined with empirical research and chemical or physical analysis helps us, in turn, understand the techniques used by Bruegel and his fellow painters. As in other branches of material research and in medicine, imaging techniques within and outside the visual spectrum allow for greater understanding of paintings' structural composition and condition. Furthermore, the condition of an artwork is deduced from knowledge of material degradation or ageing processes. It goes without saying that in all this, modern technology plays an increasingly important role. Therefore, for traditional connoisseurship not only the sophistication of the technology used, but mostly the very bulk of works from artists that have been technically analyzed, is of great value in making well-argued statements on attribution. Fortunately, in the last decade technical art historians and conservators have paid increasingly more attention to Pieter Bruegel the Elder.[19]

The imaging techniques used for the investigation of this painting include *digital photography* in very high resolution (126 Mp at 300 ppi), obtained by merging a set of 9 overlapping photographs taken with a professional digital reflex camera.[20] The photographs are color corrected by dedicated software. This technique allows for close-up visual inspection of the condition of the artwork and also facilitates in-depth stylistic analysis, of even small details. *Ultraviolet-induced visible fluorescence photography* (UIVFP) has as purpose to inspect the surface condition of varnish and to locate ancient overpaint. When inducing ultraviolet radiation on an object, different materials become visible due to differences in fluorescence. This way, retouching as well as overpaint can be distinguished from original paint. On the other side of the visible wavelengths, *infrared reflectography* (IRR) makes the preparatory drawing underneath the paint layers, the so-called 'underdrawing' visible, as well as damage and past conservation interventions. As in medical applications, *X-ray radiography* (XR) allows one to visualize the construction of the support, the spatial distribution of heavy elements (e.g. metals such as lead or mercury) present in the preparatory and paint layers, and damage.

For chemical analysis, we use mostly non-invasive techniques, meaning that no samples have to be taken and thus that the analysis does not damage the paint surface.[21] Analytical techniques used include 'portable X-ray fluorescence spectrometry' (pXRF). An

X-ray beam of circular shape with a surface of approximately 3 x 3 mm^2 is aimed at the paint surface. The secondary energy that is released subsequently is captured by a sensor and converted into a graph of energy levels (a spectrum), typical for the chemical elements present in the irradiated spot. This analytical technique makes the identification of chemical elements in the preparation and pigment layers possible. When molecular identification was needed, we used *micro raman spectroscopy*. Here a laser beam with a small spot size is aimed at an extremely tiny sample obtained by rubbing gently on the paint layer with a cotton Q-tip. The laser excites the molecules, which vibration can be captured by a sensor. This signal is converted into a spectrum, which is typical for a particular molecule. This method allows us to distinguish specific materials (e.g. pigments) on a molecular level, and not, as is with pXRF, only its constituting elements.

Support

As seen earlier, Karel van Mander stated that Pieter Bruegel the Elder painted both on canvas and on panel, and indeed, paintings by him on both supports have been preserved. *Dancing Peasants at a St. Sebastian's Kermis* was painted on a panel consisting of three horizontal boards of Baltic oak. It had been known at least since the early 15th century that oak from the Baltic region was much more stable than local Flemish wood types as it was less subject to deformation.[22] These stable qualities of Baltic oak have been confirmed by modern material science and wood biology. It is telling that artisan wood workers about 500 years ago possessed such an advanced knowledge about the materials they worked with. Indeed, Baltic oak was used nearly exclusively as a wooden painting support between the 15th and 16th century in the northwestern parts of Europe.[23]

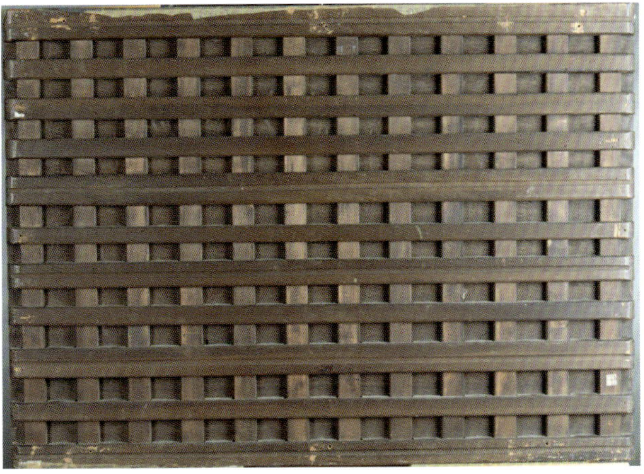

19. Reverse of the panel of ill. pp. 18 –19 © UGent, Gicas, 2018

It was customary to mount the wooden boards in their longest direction, following their grain. Thus a horizontal format, as our painting, consists of horizontal planks.

During the 16th century, full oak boards for panel painting usually had a width between 25-29 cm (roughly 1 ft).[24] The average width was a consequence of the way boards were split quarterly from the tree trunk, i.e. along the radius of the section. This can be deduced from the medullary rays that are visible at the reverse of the panel (ill. 19) and the growth rings that stand more or less perpendicular to the short ends of the board. Although more material was lost when the wood was radially cut, professionals commonly knew that it would warp less than tangentially cut planks.[25] As can be observed, indeed, the panel of the painting *Dancing Peasants at a St. Sebastian's Kermis* has remained flat over the ages.

The panel is 76.2 to 76.3 cm (2 ft 6 in to 2 ft $6^{3}/_{64}$ in) in height and 104.4 to 104.5 cm (3 ft $5^{7}/_{64}$ in to 3 ft $5^{9}/_{64}$ in) wide. The three planks have a maximum width of 29.4 – 28.2 – 18.6 cm ($11^{37}/_{64}$ – $11^{7}/_{64}$ – $7^{21}/_{64}$ in) respectively. The planks have a slightly irregular width, with dimensions varying from c. 1 to 2 cm ($^{25}/_{64}$ to $^{25}/_{32}$ in) between the left and

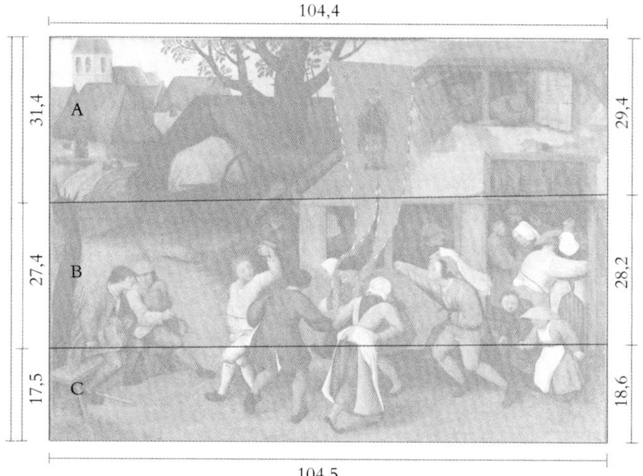

20. Schematic representation of panel construction of ill. pp. 18 –19 with detailed dimensions © UGent, Gicas, 2018

the right end. Such slanted boards are unusual because they are more difficult to attach to one another when producing a panel. However, in Pieter Bruegel the Elder's oeuvre planks sawn in such a fashion are found in other cases, such as in the *Tower of Babel*, *The Return of the Herd*, *Christ Carrying the Cross*, *The Conversion of St. Paul* and *The Birdnester* (all Vienna, Kunsthistorisches Museum).[26] It seems that Bruegel had his panels delivered by a panel maker who often worked in this peculiar way.

The thickness of the boards was relative to the length, usually between 0.8 - 3 cm ($^{5}/_{16}$ – $1^{3}/_{16}$ in), as it is logical that larger planks used to produce larger panels needed more dimensional stability than smaller ones. The planks of our painting have an average thickness of 0.5 cm ($^{13}/_{64}$ in). Probably in the early 20th century, the reverse was planed down in order to attach a cradle (visually identified as beech). The cradle consists of 12 vertical sliding and 16 horizontal fixed slats (of which 5 glued one next to the other at the height of the panel joins). Most panels from the 16th century have been reinforced at a later date with blocks, slates, and as of the 19th century onwards often with complete cradles, as is the case here. When these supporting features were applied, the wooden support had to be planed down. Therefore, panels from the 15th and 16th century seldom retain their original thickness, and often lost valuable inscription

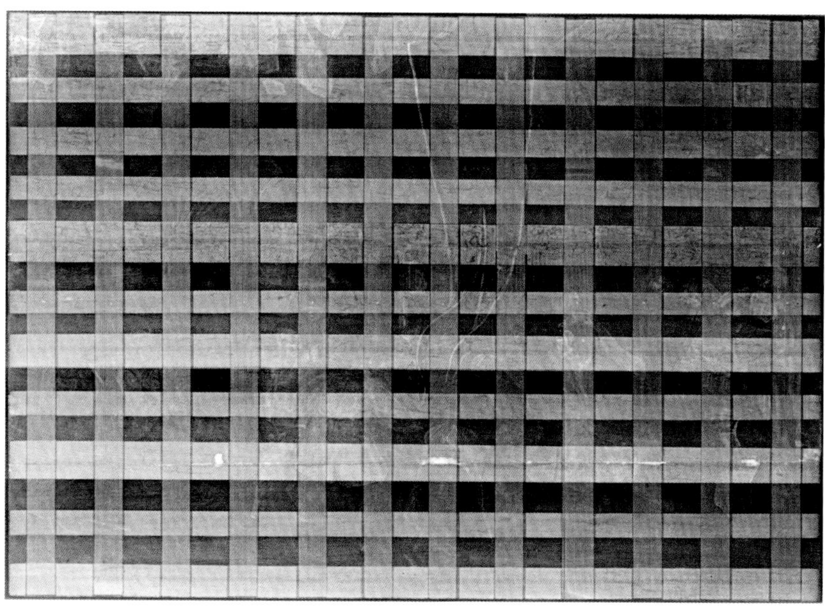

21. X-ray image of ill. pp. 18 –19 with detail of dowel © UGent, Gicas, 2018

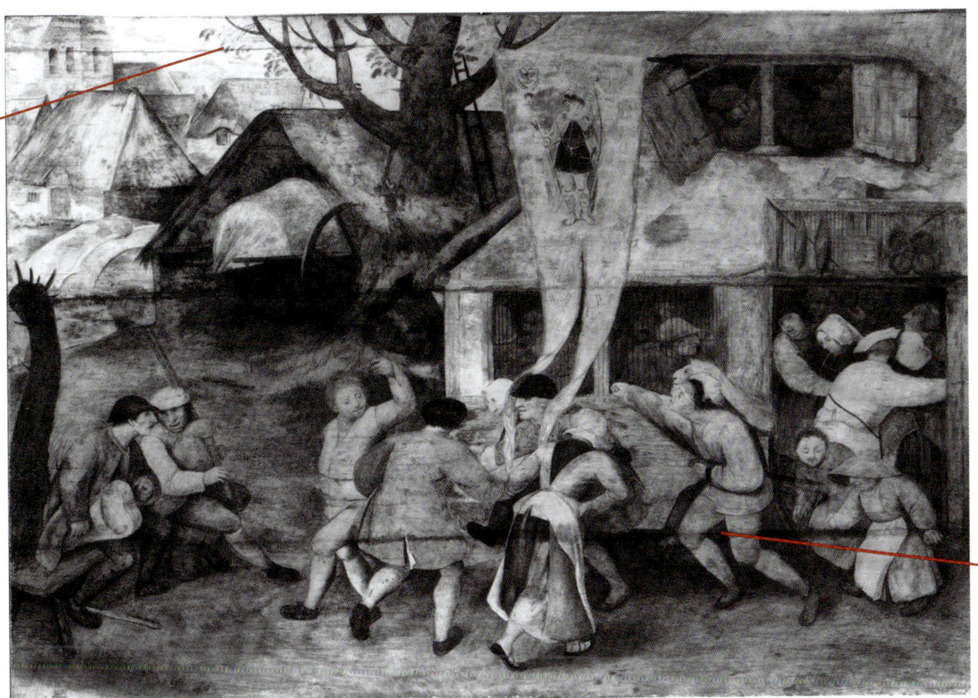

22. IRR of ill. pp. 18 –19 © UGent, Gicas, 2018

and collector's marks that figured on the original backside.

As can be seen in the X-ray image, the planks are butt joined with dowels (ill. 21, 24), as observed in other paintings by Pieter Bruegel I.[27] This technique of joining boards was very common in early Flemish painting. Judging from retouching along the lower join (visible in the IRR, ill. 22) and the presence of lead white visible in the X-ray image, it must have become detached at some point in time and was fixed. Although it has also been retouched, the upper join has suffered less.

The technical images show a horizontal crack running at the top left from at about 4 cm (1 ft $^{37}/_{64}$ in) from the top to about the middle of the panel. During the recent treatment, this crack has been carefully retouched. The sides are rather regular; the corners slightly worn. It seems that the panel retains its original dimensions as no traces of sawing can be found along the edges. The panel has no unpainted borders and shows no signs of warp. The wood has been infected in a few areas by xylophages, as shown by corridors in the X-ray image. However, the damage has been treated and stabilized. After the latest treatment, the support is in stable condition and the joins barely visible.

Ground and Priming Layers

Wooden panels were prepared and sanded as to obtain an even white surface, suitable to apply paint layers that properly adhere to it. In Northern Europe, and especially in the Low Countries, nearly always chalk (calcium carbonate) mixed with animal glue was used for that purpose. In the Mediterranean, chalk was usually substituted with gypsum (calcium sulfate). In other words, the identification of this ground layer allows localizing a painting.

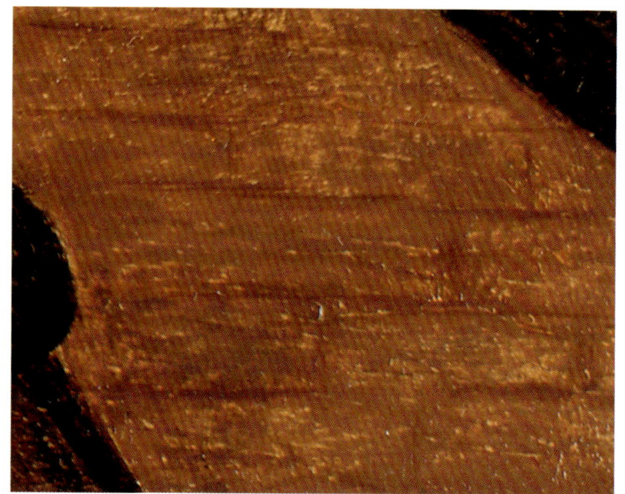

23. Wall with brownish imprimatura showing through
Detail of ill. pp. 18–19 © UGent, Gicas, 2018

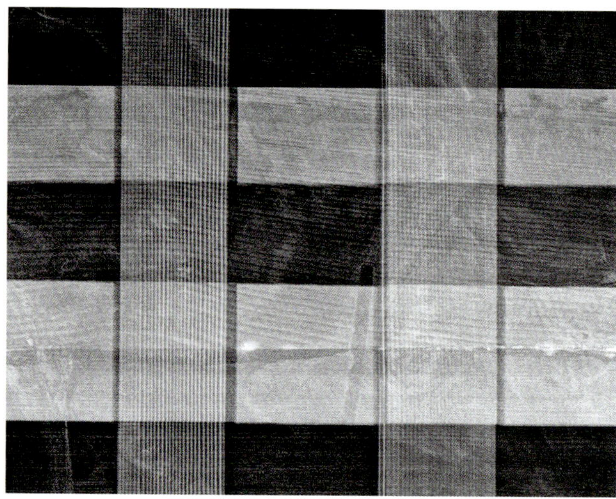

24. X-ray image of ill. pp. 18–19 concentrated in the grain of the wood lead white was mixed in this imprimatura © UGent, Gicas, 2018

When looking at a sample of such a calcium carbonate ground under a scanning electron microscopy (SEM), tiny marine algae, typical for calcite, can be seen. In the *Dancing Peasants at a St. Sebastian's Kermis*, X-ray fluorescence and raman spectroscopic analyses revealed calcite ($CaCO_3$), deriving from the ground layer, which was most likely mixed with animal glue (medium not analyzed), as is usual in Flemish paintings of the time. The ground is applied on the entire surface of the support up to all four edges. It has a proper adhesion and is generally in good condition. After cleaning and before retouching, it was well visible in several abraded areas.

In Pieter Bruegel I's time, the ground layer was often colored with a pigmented layer, called 'imprimatura' or 'pigmented isolation layer'. Some authors call this, following Karel Van Mander, 'priming' (*primuersel*).[28] Actually, Bruegel was one of the first artists to apply such intermediate layers systematically. Judged from the broad stripes coarsely applied with a wide flat harsh brush in different directions and unrelated to the actual figuration, the painting has such an imprimatura, as is found in most paintings by Pieter Bruegel the Elder.[29] With the naked eye it can be observed that the imprimatura has a brownish ochre hue (ill. 23).[30] Moreover, the whitish gaze detectible in the X-ray image, especially concentrated in the grain of the wood, indicates that some lead white was mixed in this imprimatura (ill. 24).

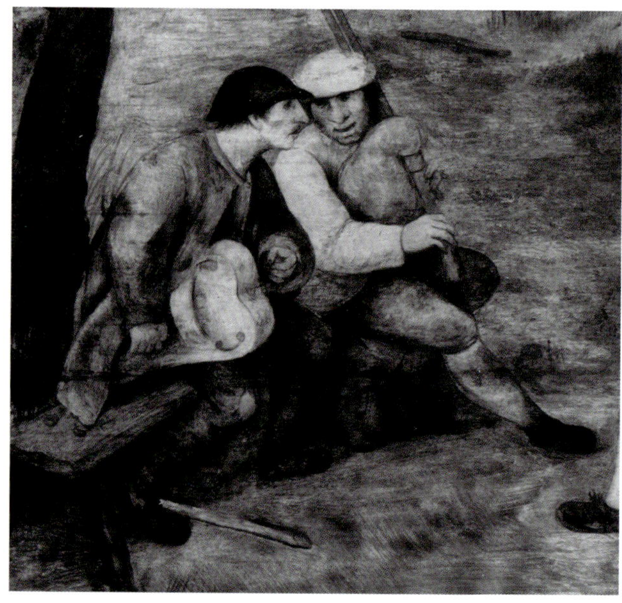

25. IRR of ill. 2 showing black stripes of imprimatura in foreground
© UGent, Gicas, 2018

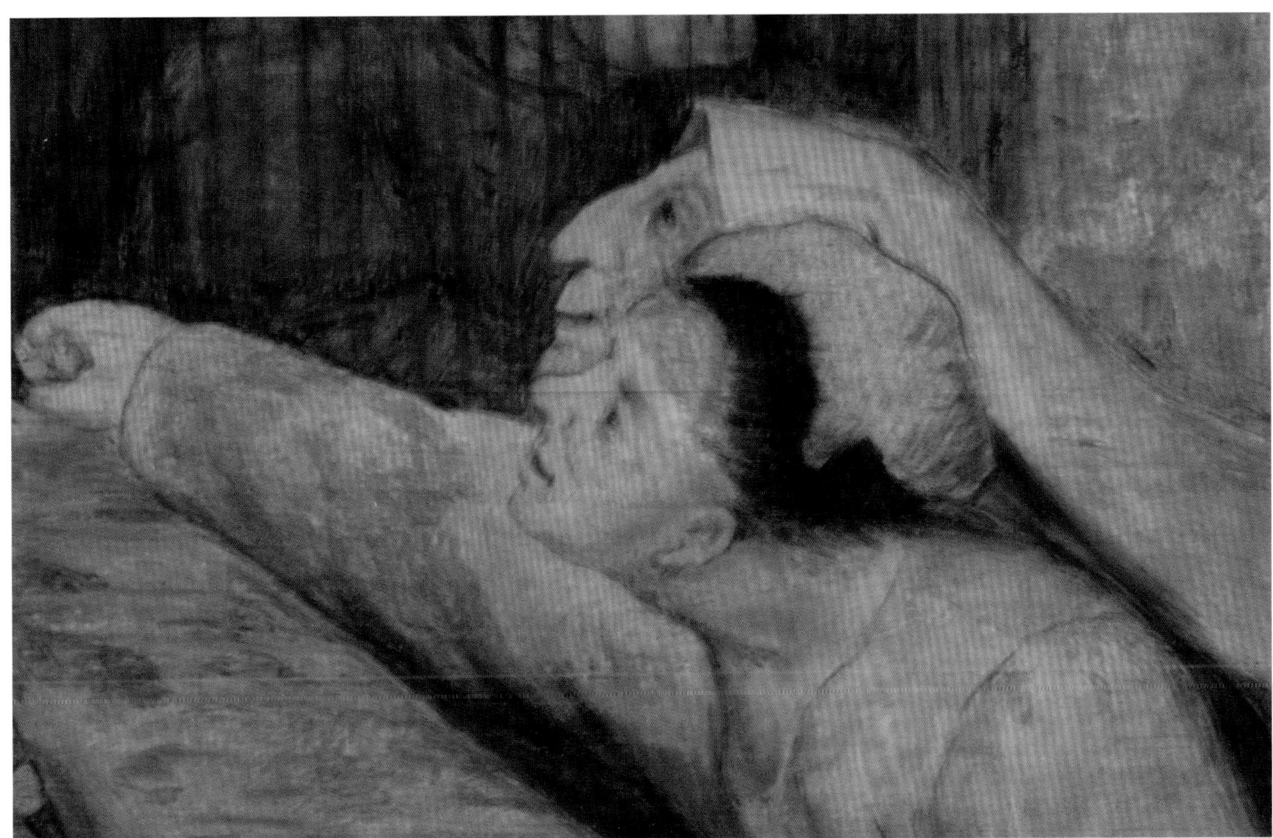

26. Layered image (80% IRR – 20%VIS) showing tilting back of woman's head and change in form of man's bonnet. Detail of ill. pp. 18-19 © UGent, Gicas, 2018

This is confirmed by the identification of lead in several obtained chemical spectra.[31]

The broad black stripes deriving from a wide brush that can be discerned in the IRR (ill. 25), also point to carbon black in the mixture of the imprimatura. The raman-spectroscopic results for many measuring points indicate indeed the presence of carbon black. The imprimatura served two functions. First, it regulated the absorption of oil by the ground. Second, it provided a unifying tone for parts or the whole of the composition. Very characteristic for Pieter Bruegel I's painting technique is that it grants an optical suggestion of vibrating hues and in many areas, it remains uncovered functioning as a middle tone for economically rendered textures.

Underdrawing

It was common practice in early Flemish painting to draw the entire composition on the prepared ground prior to the painting process. Usually a carbon-holding material, either a dry medium (e.g. black chalk, charcoal) or a liquid one (e.g. certain black inks), was employed. Such carbon-based drawing materials absorb infrared radiation while other materials such as iron gall ink and inorganic pigments reflect it. Therefore, infrared reflectography (IRR) makes the preparatory drawing of a painting visible.

Although the paint layers are fairly thinly applied, the underdrawing is difficult to see with the naked eye. Revealed by IRR (ill. 26), it can be observed that it establishes only most contours in figuration, architecture and other compositional elements. Therefore, it may be safely assumed that the underdrawing has been traced — probably from a 1:1 cartoon — and reinforced in a liquid material, likely to be identified as black carbonaceous ink.

Deviations in the underdrawing from the finally painted composition indicate where the artists made compositional changes during the creative process. In comparison to the underdrawing of our painting, nearly no shifts of form are detectable in the paint layer, which is evidently a result of the tracing transferal technique. Following a systematic comparison between the underdrawing and the final painting stage,[32] only one significant shift could be discovered: the head of the older dancing woman in front of the house was tilted back and her exaggerated hooked nose reduced already during the underdrawing phase (ill. 26).[33] The form of her young companion's bonnet was changed during the painting process. This indicates that these changes were part of Bruegel's creative process, which seems to indicate that the painting is an original composition and no copy. It is significant to note that Marten Van Cleve followed precisely Bruegel's final painted forms in his copy.

As the darker contours often have been reinforced in the final painting process, the underdrawing is usually covered and therefore invisible to the naked eye. As Bruegel used black in the different phases of the painting process, the underdrawing is always difficult to distinguish in his works. This type of underdrawing described here adheres entirely to the workshop practice identified in other Bruegel the Elder's paintings. This practice was also noted in other unanimously attributed signed works, such as *Mad Meg* (a.k.a. *Dulle Griet*, Antwerp, Mayer Van den Bergh Museum)[34] and the *Triumph of Dead* (Madrid, Museo del Prado).[35] In other paintings, Bruegel worked only in a dry medium (probably black chalk), sometimes limited to carefully laying out the contours (such as in the Viennese *Children' Games*, *Battle between Carnaval and Lent*, *Christ Carrying the Cross* and *The Birdnester*). In other cases, the underdrawing is more freely sketched, such as e.g. in the Viennese *Tower of Babel* and Season paintings.[36] In the recent literature, it has been convincingly argued that Pieter Bruegel often made a pre-established design on a 1:1 scale of the eventual painting. This drawing was subsequently traced on the support of the painting.[37] This explains the presence of traced underdrawings with very few compositional changes in his oeuvre. This carefully planned working routine could be related to Bruegel's choice of painting very thinly. In this '*alla prima*' technique visible changes between the underdrawing and the final painting layers were to be avoided.[38]

Pigments

The pigment palette of Northern artists in the 16th century differed slightly from that of Italian artists, but was equally restricted, usually to minerals and organic materials that were more or less easily available. The pigments used have been identified by XRF- and Raman spectrometry measurements. They all correspond to the standard Flemish 16th-century palette in general and to that found in other paintings by Pieter Bruegel the Elder.[39] Typically, lead white is the only white used in this painting. In the flesh tones lead-white was mixed with the red pigment vermillion. Also the red banner was painted in vermillion. The yellow, such as in the area in the house to the right of the flag could not be identified as it is probably of organic composition (e.g. yellow lake); by mixing it with red ochre an orange hue was obtained.[40] Brown and ochre tones all contain iron oxide, and thus derive from earth pigments.

The black in the dark background behind the figures on the 2nd floor could not be identified analytically but seems to consist of carbon black judged from its absorption in infrared. The detected iron peaks in the spectrum, deriving from the brown paint used in the wood of the house, indicates probably an earth pigment, while in the tree also some vermillion is detected. The dancing man seen on his back in the middle foreground wears a blue shirt, consisting of azurite. Azurite is a rather expensive pigment, which Pieter Bruegel often substituted by the much cheaper, but very unstable smalt, like in the Antwerp *Dulle Griet* or the Viennese *Peasants' Kermis*, where it discolored irreversibly to a dull greyish hue.[41] The presence of azurite may indicate high exigencies on the part of the original commissioner of the painting. The azurite-based blue shirt of the dancing man was partially overpainted with Prussian blue, which is a late 18th-century pigment. In the sleeve of this dancing man also red ochre (hematite) was detected.

Paint Layers

Pigments were grinded and mixed with oil. Usually linseed oil was used as a medium. The medium here was not analyzed, as there are no readily available non-destructive techniques to do so, and the results of such analyses are in these cases very predictable as oil paint on panel was the most widespread technique in the Netherlands in the 16th century. Actually, it existed along glue sized tempera paintings on canvas. However, even an untrained eye can very easily distinguish between both techniques.

By adding more medium to the pigments, paint layers could be applied translucently as 'glazes', and when less medium was added, artists could paint more opaquely. Oil paint can be applied in a sequence of drying layers or wet-in-wet. This wide range of possibilities allows for talented artists to suggest nearly every imaginable texture and material and forms a technical basis for the famous 'realism' in early Flemish painting.

The grounded support has been covered with paint layers up to the edges. Before c. 1520, Northern paintings were always painted in the frame, leaving unpainted edges at all four sides when it was removed later. This is not the case here, as this older practice had been mostly abandoned by Bruegel's time.

Varnish

Finally, paintings were varnished in order to protect the paint layers. Varnish also provides depth by saturating the oily paint layers and gives an even shine to the entire surface. The old resinous oxidized varnish has been removed recently and replaced by a synthetic resin varnish.

Condition

Currently, the condition of the painting is excellent, having undergone a substantial conservation treatment in 2017. The structure of the wooden support is flat and stable with well-glued joins between the three constituting planks. The paint surface is absolutely clean and adheres very well, showing no blisters. The varnish is equally applied with a uniform shine.

Before this treatment much retouching and often unnecessarily large overpainting disfigured the painting. This was the result of one or more clumsily executed restorations. In the photograph published by Friedländer

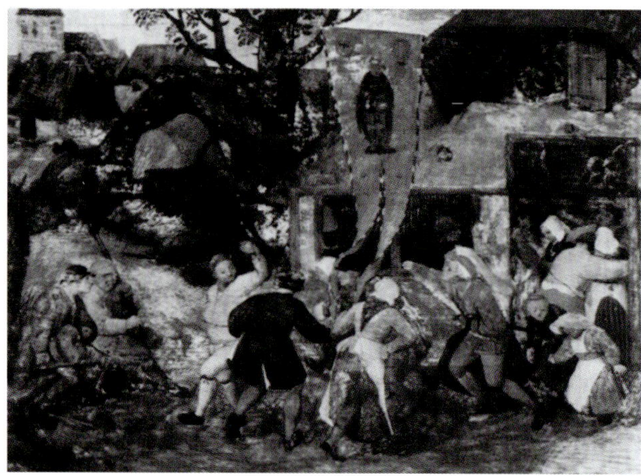

27. Photograph published by Max J. Friedländer

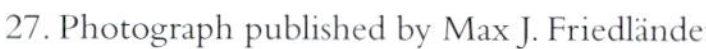

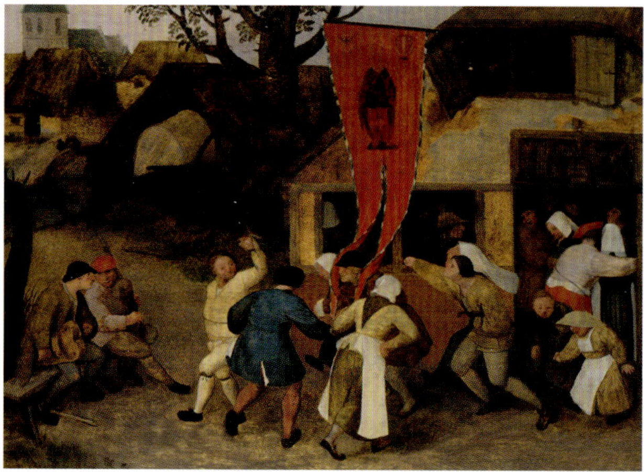

28. State before conservation treatment, 2016

(ill. 27),[42] one can notice that the paint over the joins, and especially the lower one, had become detached, as is often the case. Moreover, the surface has been abraded in some areas, probably due to overzealous cleaning of the very thinly applied glazes, so typical for Pieter Bruegel the Elder.

This explains why most people who saw the work overpainted as it was (ill. 28), could not recognize the hand of Pieter Bruegel the Elder, in contrast to Friedländer, who knew it in its 'naked' state.

During the recent conservation, all disfiguring overpaint was carefully removed, except for the Prussian blue on the jacket of the dancing man seen on his back in the middle, where complete removal was judged to be too hazardous to harm the original azurite paint layer. Furthermore, the abraded fragile earth tones were carefully painted in with integrated retouching in water colors and egg tempera and finishes in resinous varnish. The same holds for faded contour lines that were reinforced, based on the underdrawing, making use of the IRR-documents. The latter was necessary to regain the legibility of the composition. No reconstruction of figurative elements was necessary. This fine treatment was performed by Paul Bouquette, a well-known Brussels based painting conservator, specialized in 16th- and 17th-century Flemish painting. He estimates the amount of retouching at about 25% of the painted surface and concentrated mainly in the earth tones and along the joins. This is well below what is deemed theoretically acceptable in professional conservation ethics, and far less than what often occurs on the art market.

Painting Technique and Stylistic Analysis

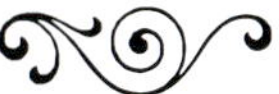

Pieter Bruegel the Elder's painting technique is easily recognizable, as he worked in an extremely economic manner, often letting the colored ground shine through the upper layers, which by themselves were often very thinly applied as glazes. Quickly applied brush strokes are often very well visible in these transparent layers. After the application of the ground, imprimatura and the underdrawing, he applied preliminary translucent paint layers in broad zones, blocking out lighter areas. This way, he determined the dark-light contrast in the composition early on in the creative process. In dark zones this layer usually contained carbon black pigment, which registers well in infrared, but as stated before, interferes with the underdrawing, making the latter often difficult to distinguish. This preliminary paint layer is found here in most of the ground, the dark clothes, the trees, the darkest part of the barn and the interior of the inn visible through the windows.

The economic paint technique and simple layer structure can be observed in the depiction of earth and architecture, built up by large thinly applied surfaces consisting often of dappled earth pigments, superimposed by small quickly drawn lines to suggest textures such as bricks, wooden planks or thatched roofs (ill. 29). On the other hand, white parts of the costumes and some facial features were painted more opaquely in lead-white. After that, the artist applied shadows, enhancing the modeling of the figures, and by casting shadows, the three-dimensional suggestion.

Often contours were reinforced with small brownish or black lines. Forms were often accentuated by white highlights, quickly applied with great dexterity. Due to the thin application of many paint layers, cracks are only visible in the lead white containing areas.

This economic, quick and often very thin painting technique, called '*alla prima*', in which the vibrating imprimatura plays a fundamental role, results in patchy dabbed zones with much tonal differentiation. This way Bruegel often suggested more than he actually painted. Through modern insights in neurological processing of vision, we know now that our brain supplements what has been consciously omitted. Bruegel must have come to this conclusion by pure empirical observation. Such an innovation in painting technique must have been considered as what we would coin

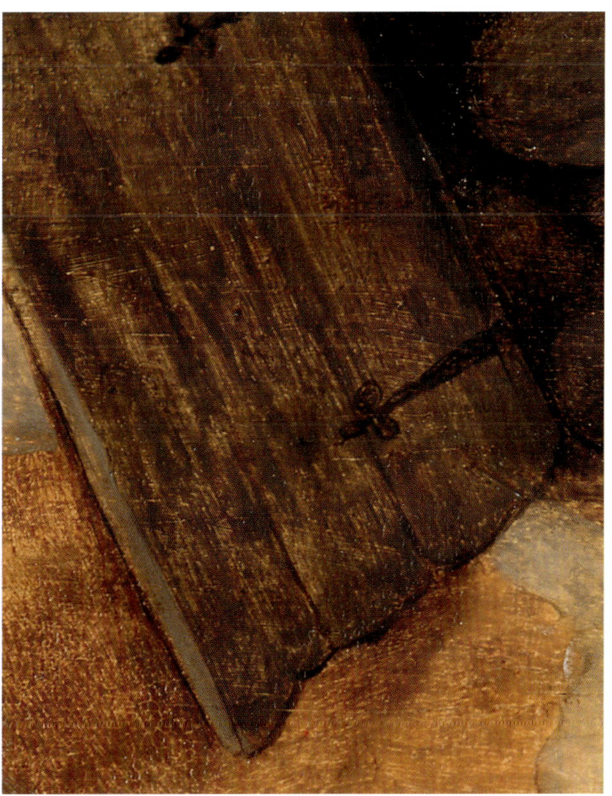

29. Detail of ill. pp. 18-19 © UGent, Gicas, 2018

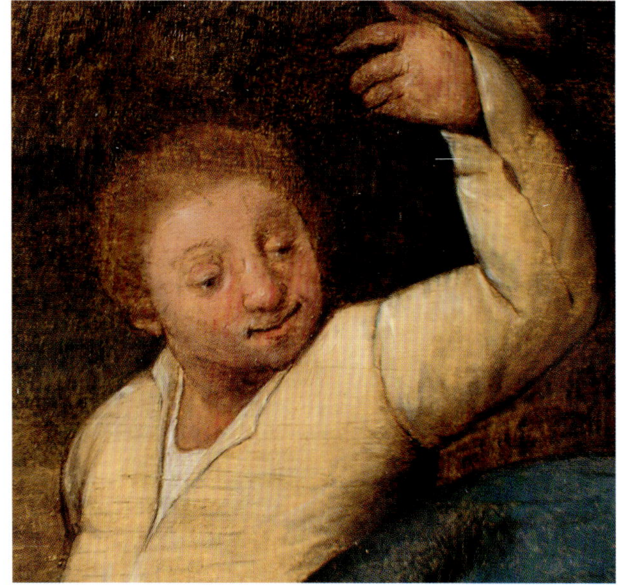

30. Detail of ill. pp. 18-19 © UGent, Gicas, 2018

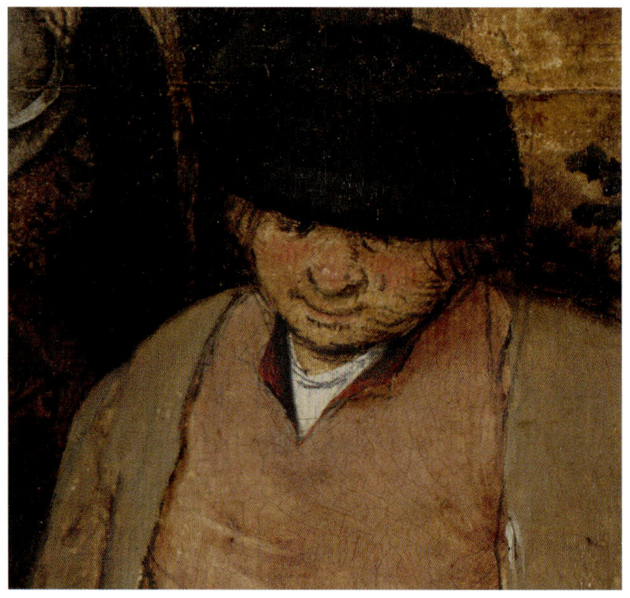

31. Detail of the young man, Detroit, Detroit Institute of Arts © Bridgeman Images

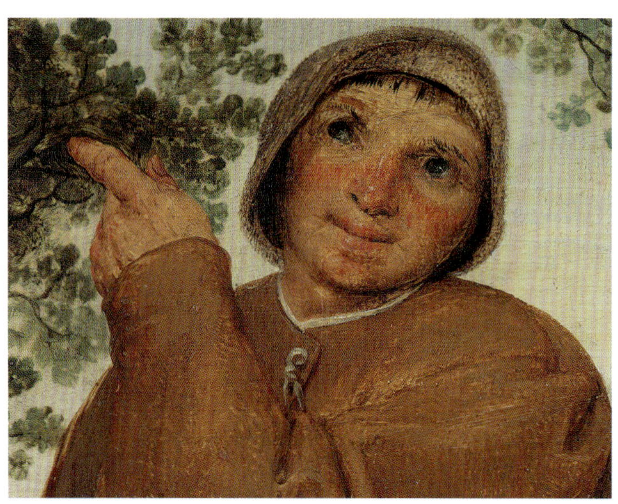

32. Detail of *BIRDNESTER*, Vienna, Kunsthistorisches Museum ©Vienna, Kunsthistorisches Museum

today as '*avant garde*'. It clarifies both Ortelius' statement that he painted more than what could be painted, and was presumably criticized as too revolutionary by Lucas d'Heere in his negative remarks on 'Quidam'.

Pieter Bruegel the Elder's works show some idiosyncratic characteristics in figure types. Some have round caricature-like faces with prominent features. The blond rather corpulent young man, leading the dance, has such a round face. The lighter parts of his face are indicated with a pinkish opaque hue, while in the transparent darker areas, the brownish imprimatura can still be noticed, which is the case in the neck and the typical round eye sockets and dark eyes. Some features of the face are sketched in dark brown lines. A hint of red glaze is used to mark the upper lips, and black or dark lines suggest eyes and nostrils. Vibrancy and shadows were suggested with brown hatching. The highlights are indicated with quickly placed short brushstrokes of lead white. Besides the dark eyes in round sockets, conveying an impression of dopey naiveté, he has a flat wide nose. His earlobe is just visible. He seems to have a counter part in the young man standing next to a tree at the right of the *Wedding Dance* in Detroit (ill. 31) or even the peasant in the Munich *Birdnester* (ill. 32), while he equally resembles the richly dressed lying man in *Cocaigne* (Munich, Alte Pinakothek, ill. 34).

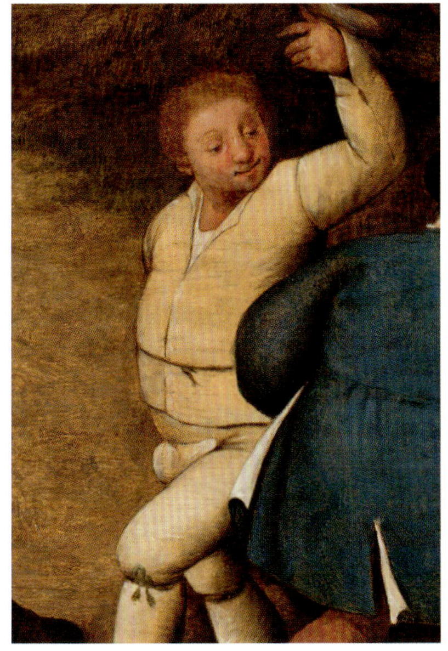

33. Detail of ill. pp. 18-19 © UGent, Gicas, 2018

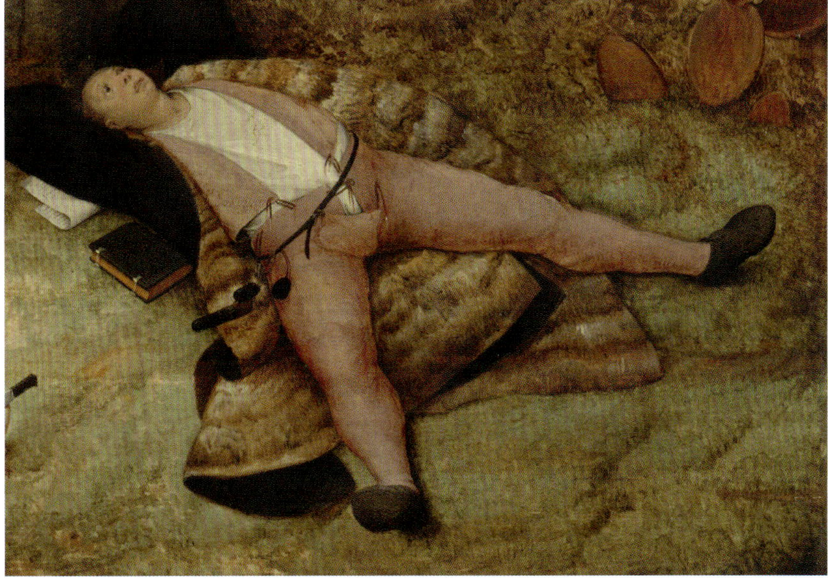

34. Detail of PIETER BRUEGEL I, *COCAIGNE*, oil on panel, Munich, Alte Pinakothek © bpk-Bildagentur

Middle aged and older men, like the dancing man under the banner, the man standing frontally in the inn's doorway or the bagpiper have large noses, sometimes hooked, and, remarkably very often lack a phyltrum, the vertical indentation in the middle area of the upper lip. They all share a course and simple-minded expression. Resembling figures can be found throughout Bruegel the Elder's oeuvre (see pp. 18-19). The dancing man is similar in type to one of the guests sitting on a bench behind the table at the *Peasants' Wedding* in Vienna (ill. 36). The one in the doorway, bluntly smiling with his mouth forming a crescent and showing his bad teeth, reminds the rich man strewing roses for swines in the *Netherlandish Proverbs* (Berlin, Gemäldegalerie) (ill. 38).

Female peasant faces are painted much in the same manner as male ones, the indication of wrinkles depending of course on their age (ill. 39). Their expression is not more intelligent than that of their male counterparts. It is possible that such stock figure types were based on painted head studies ('tronies'). The physiognomic resemblance between the old dancing woman and the *Head of a Peasant Woman* (Munich, Alte Pinakothek) (ill. 40) seems to suggest such a working procedure.

The children in the right foreground imitate adult behavior like many of their age do in the famous Viennese *Peasants' Wedding* and *Children's Games* (ill. 43). Not only their squatty posture, but even the way their hands are painted in one color tone, contoured with a brown line and with rather pointed fingers, is similar. Some children, like adults in many of Bruegel's works have their faces hidden or partly covered by headgear.

Pieter the Elder introduced equally in nearly all his compositions people seen from the backside (ill. 44-45). The dancing man in the blue jacket adapts the same posture as the pudding serving man in red in the *Peasants' Wedding* (Vienna, Kunsthistorisches Museum). With these figures seen from their backs,

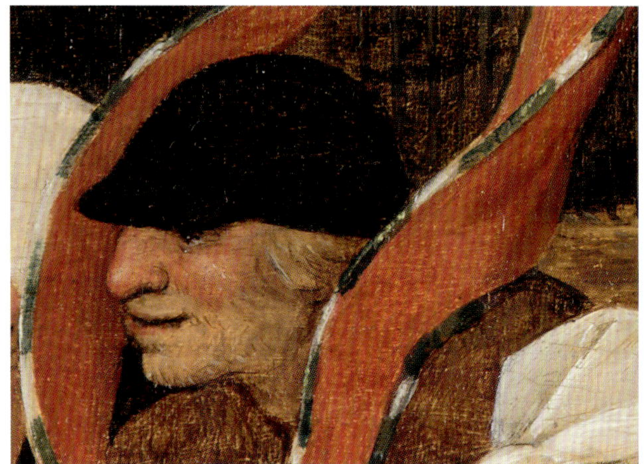

35. Detail of ill. pp. 18-19 © UGent, Gicas, 2018

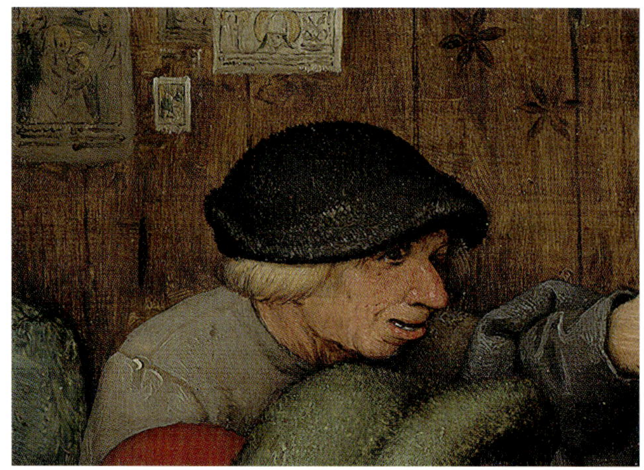

36. Detail of *PEASANTS' WEDDING*
Vienna, Kunsthistorisches Museum © Vienna, Kunsthistorisches Museum

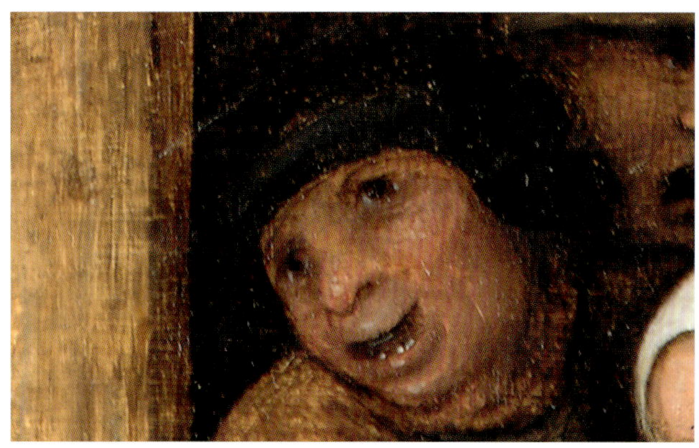

37. Detail of ill. pp. 18-19 © UGent, Gicas, 2018

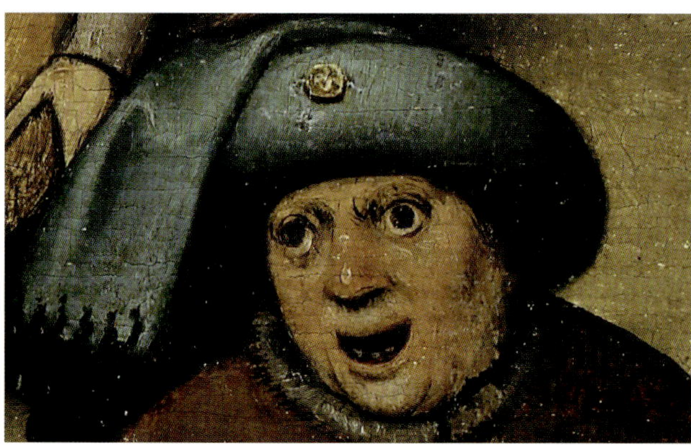

38. Detail of PIETER BRUEGEL II, *NETHERLANDISH PROVERBS*,
oil on panel, Berlin, Staatliche Museen Preussischer Kulturbesitz, Gemäldegalerie
© bpk-Bildagentur

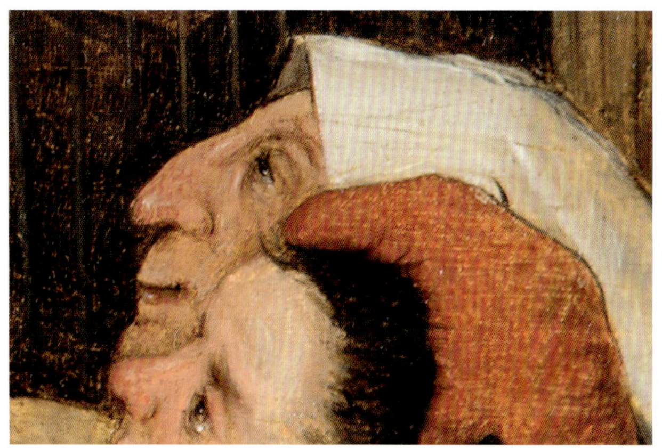

39. Detail of ill. pp. 18-19 © UGent, Gicas, 2018

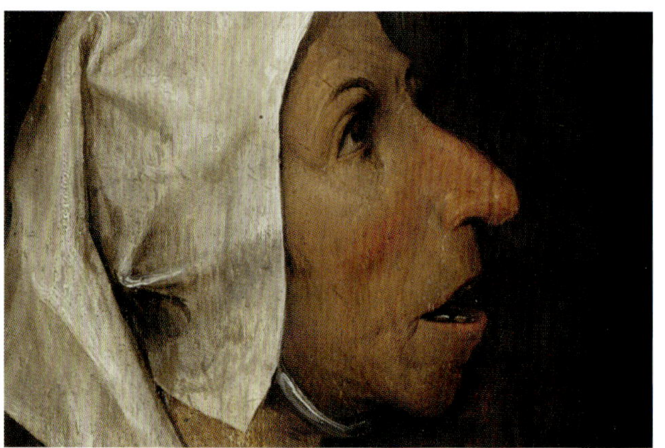

40. PIETER BRUEGEL I, *HEAD OF A PEASANT WOMAN*
oil on panel, Munich, Alte Pinakothek © bpk-Bildagentur

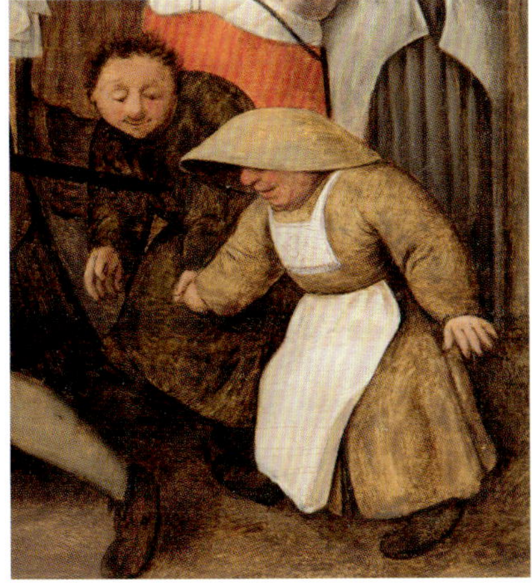

41. Detail of ill. pp. 18-19
© UGent, Gicas, 2018

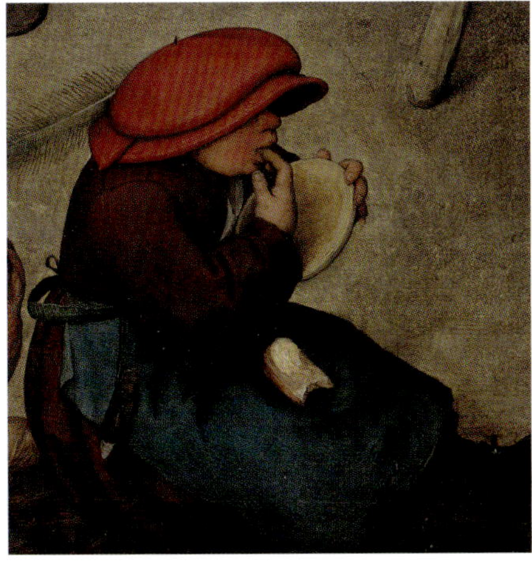

42. Detail of *PEASANTS' WEDDING*, Vienna, Kunsthistorisches Museum ©Vienna, Kunsthistorisches Museum

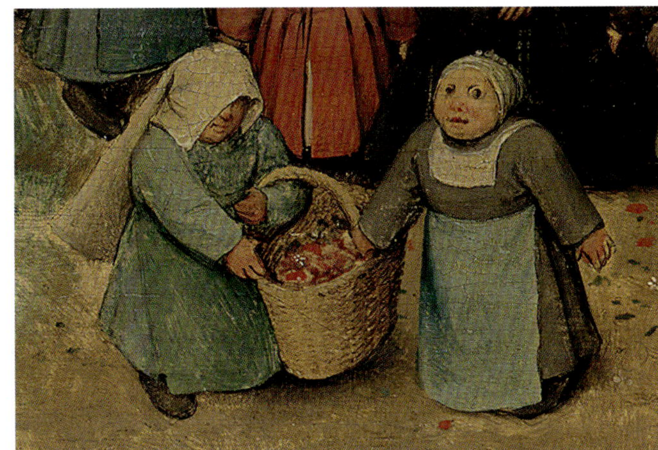

43. Detail of PIETER BRUEGEL I, *CHILDREN'S GAMES*, oil on panel, Vienna, Kunsthistorisches Museum ©Vienna, Kunsthistorisches Museum

he drew the observer in the composition, but simultaneously, it granted his works a touch of non-individuality and timelessness, as if he tried to represent what modern authors and philosophers have called 'la condition humaine'.

Something else that Bruegel mastered as no other artist, is the convincing suggestion of movement by those coarse, plump peasant people. While dancing they seem to naturally sway in an almost graceful fashion (ill. 33, 51).

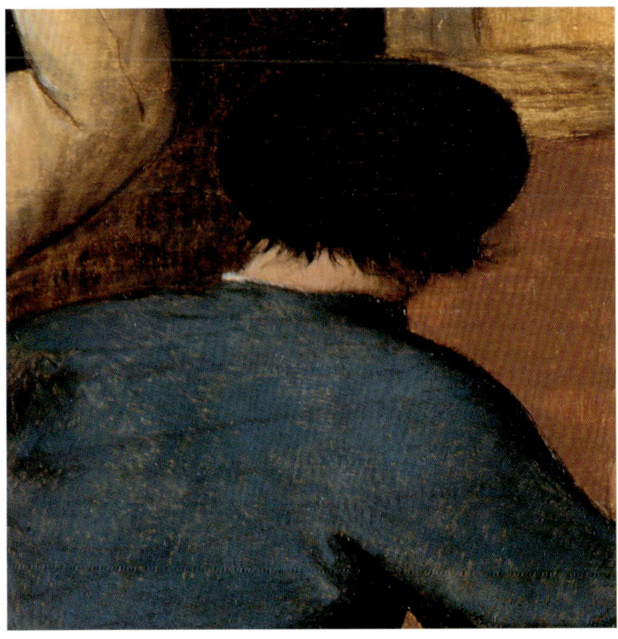

44. Detail of ill. pp. 18-19 © UGent, Gicas, 2018

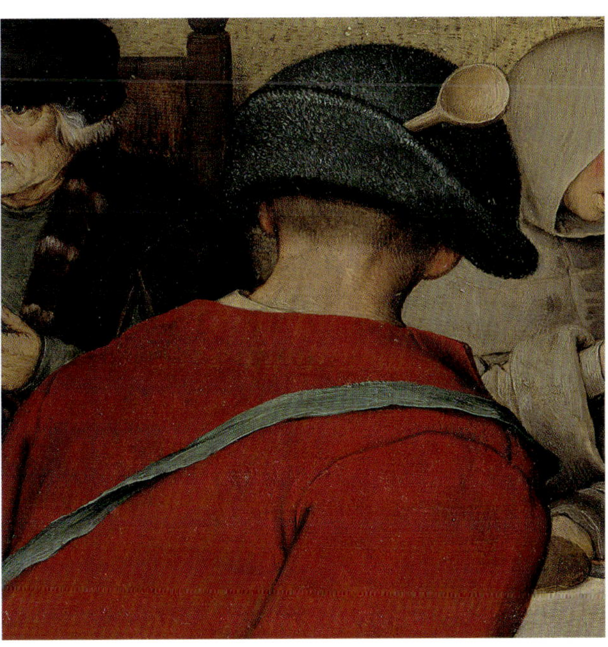

45. Detail of *PEASANTS' WEDDING*, Vienna, Kunsthistorisches Museum ©Vienna, Kunsthistorisches Museum

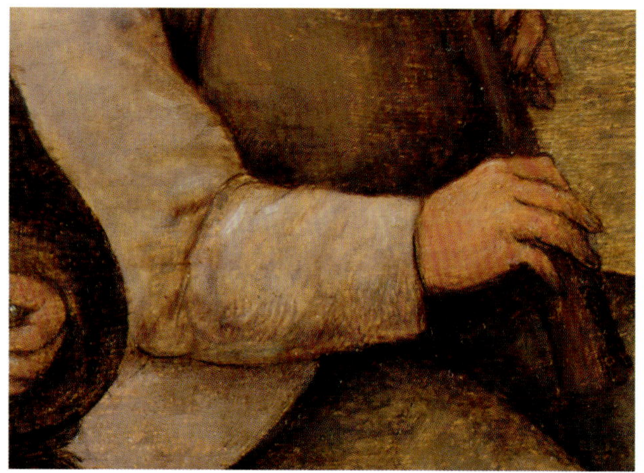

46. Detail of ill. pp. 18-19 © UGent, Gicas, 2018

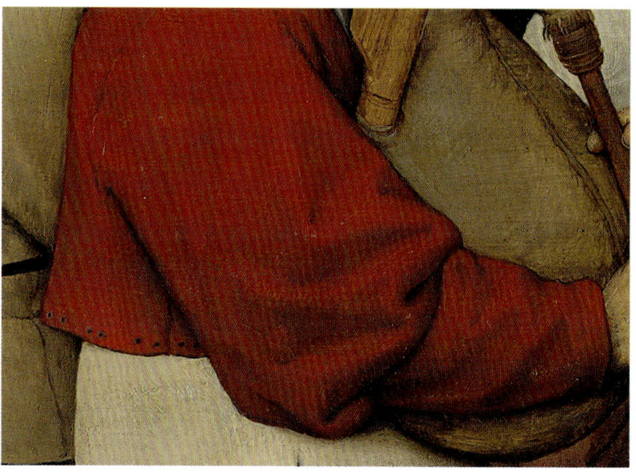

47. Detail of *PEASANTS' WEDDING*, Vienna, Kunsthistorisches Museum © Vienna, Kunsthistorisches Museum

Van Mander pointed this out already:

"He knew how to attire these men and women peasants very characteristically in Kempish or other costume, and how to express naturally that simple, peasant appearance in their dancing, toing and froing and other activities."[43]

Not one single follower was able to imitate this convincing movement of peasant folk, all drifting into the rigid stiffness of unnatural gestures. The works of Pieter the Younger are exemplary, as is by all means the copy after our painting by Marten Van Cleve, mentioned earlier.

Van Mander explicitly mentions peasants' clothing. We can indeed notice the way specific attire is painted, like e.g. the presence of parallel hatching in the shadows of the sleeves of the bagpiper and his colleague in the *Peasants' Wedding* (Vienna, Kunsthistorisches Museum) (ill. 46, 47) or the manner in which white highlights are applied on white garments (ill. 48, 49). Yet also the typology of attire is similar in our painting as in others by Pieter Bruegel the Elder. For instance, the aprons worn by women have strands attached to the corners, that are crossed in the back and tied in the front, suggested by a thin line of light paint (ill. 50, 51). Under the apron, the women wear thick, knife-pleated skirts that are shaped with very dark shadows between the pleats. Details like women's kerchiefs and the neckline of their dresses are often identical (ill. 53, 54). The same holds for leggings or stockings. On their backside often a seam is painted, either drawn in with a blunt point in wet paint or painted on with a darker color (ill. 55, 56). Because 16th-century fabrics did not have the elasticity of modern ones, hoses were tied just below the knee with a garter (ill. 57-58). The shoes with rounded tips are painted with different overlapping brushstrokes, often creating diffused contours or double outlines.

Evidently, such small corresponding details also appear in other features. The way the vertical rods are tied in the window behind the banner appeared earlier in a window in the *Netherlandish Proverbs* (Berlin, Gemäldegalerie) (ill. 59, 60). The bark of a tree is suggested by dabbling dark brown and black tones on a lighter brown glaze, while leaves are imitated by oval green dabs applied with a hard-bristled brush (ill. 61), much in a similar way as the large tree in which the birdnester climbs (Vienna, Kunsthistorisches Museum)(ill. 62). Like our painting,

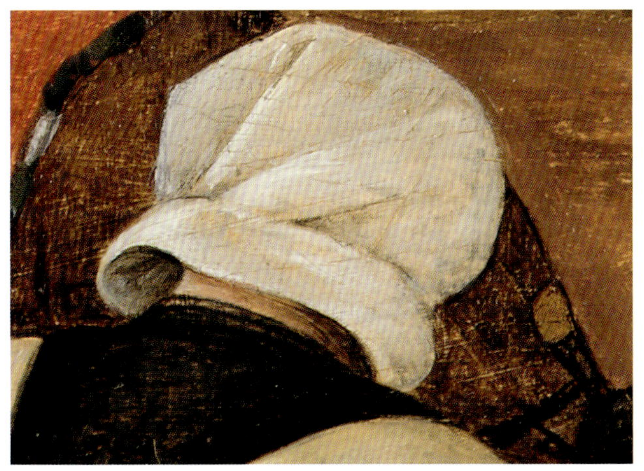

48. Detail of ill. pp. 18-19 © UGent, Gicas, 2018.

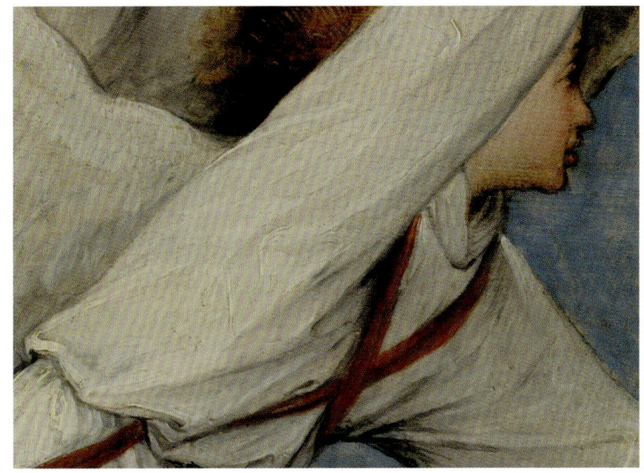

49. Detail of *PIETER BRUEGEL I, FALL OF THE REBEL ANGELS* (Brussels, Koninklijke Musea voor Schone Kunsten van België) © kik-irpa Brussels

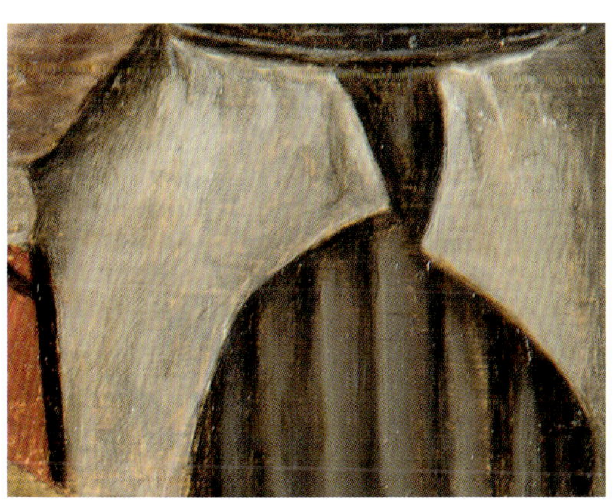

50. Detail of ill. pp. 18-19 © UGent, Gicas, 2018

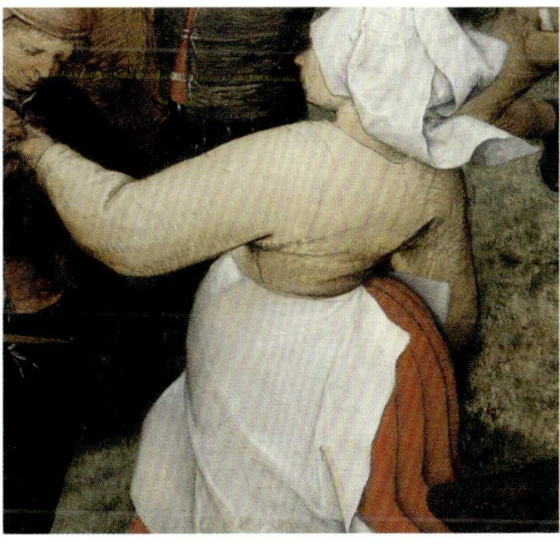

51. Detail of *THE WEDDING DANCE*, Detroit, Detroit Institute of Arts © Bridgeman Images

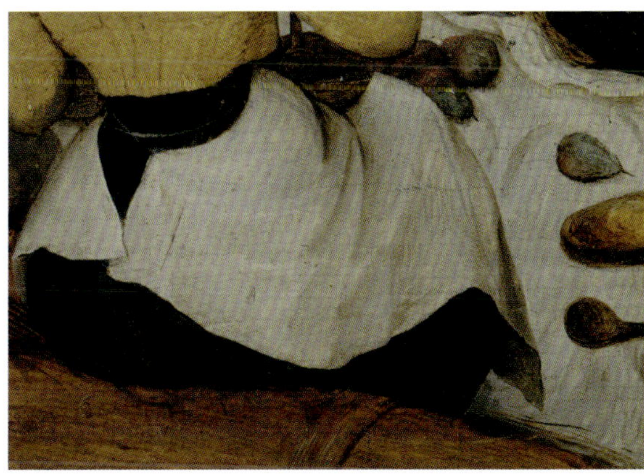

52. Detail of PIETER BRUEGEL I, *THE HARVESTERS* oil on panel, New York, The Metropolitan Museum of Art © The Metropolitan Museum of Art, New York

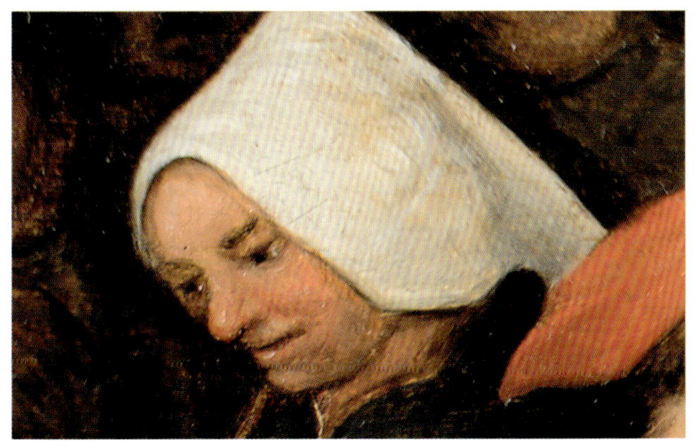

53. Detail of ill. pp. 18-19 © UGent, Gicas, 2018

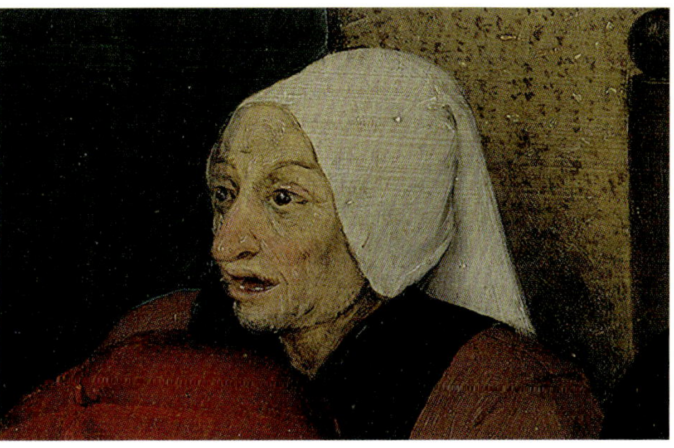

54. Detail of *PEASANTS' WEDDING*, Vienna, Kunsthistorisches Museum © Vienna, Kunsthistorisches Museum

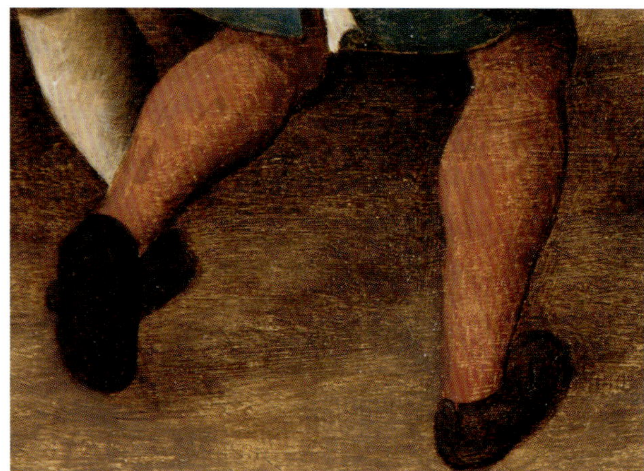

55. Detail of ill. pp. 18-19 © UGent, Gicas, 2018

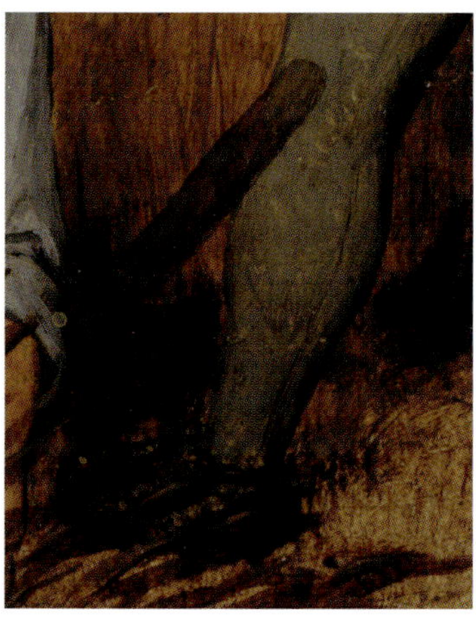

56. Detail of *THE HARVESTERS*
New York, The Metropolitan Museum of Art
© The Metropolitan Museum of Art, New York

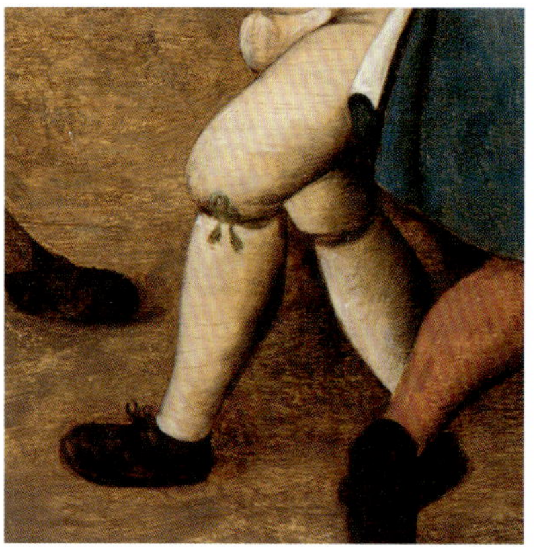

57. Detail of ill. pp. 18-19: © UGent, Gicas, 2018

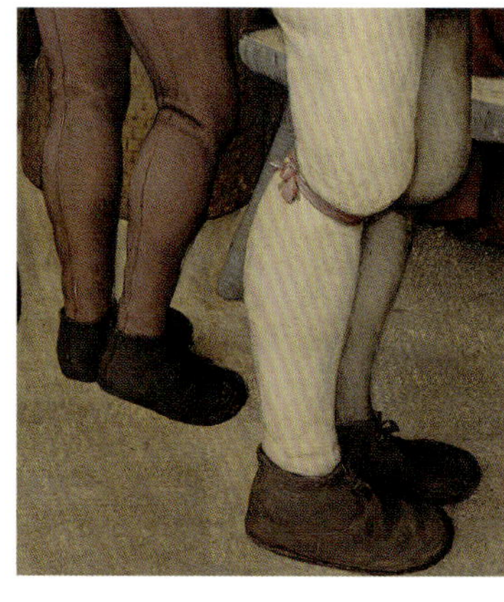

58. Detail of *PEASANTS' WEDDING*,
Vienna, Kunsthistorisches Museum
© Vienna, Kunsthistorisches Museum

The Harvesters (New York, The Metropolitan Museum of Art) and *The Sermon of St. John the Baptist* (Budapest, Museum of Fine Arts) show short vertical brown or green dashes as suggestion of grass and straw stubble (ill. 63).

This chapter has demonstrated that not only similar typology of figures, materials and objects in *Dancing Peasants at a St. Sebastian's Kermis* can be found throughout Pieter Bruegel the Elder's oeuvre, but also the manner in which they are painted is very similar. Although similarities can be found, it seems that Bruegel's style, type of underdrawing, coloristic preferences and even degree of finish was related to the subject matter of each painting and that it cannot be described in terms of a linear chronological stylistic development.[44] This phenomenon explains the coloristic differences between the two versions of the Tower of Babel, as well as the incredible difference in degree of finish between the loosely painted *Misanthrope* (Naples, Museo Nazionale di Capodimonte) and the highly detailed *Magpie on the Gallows* (Darmstadt, Hessisches Landesmuseum), both painted in 1568.

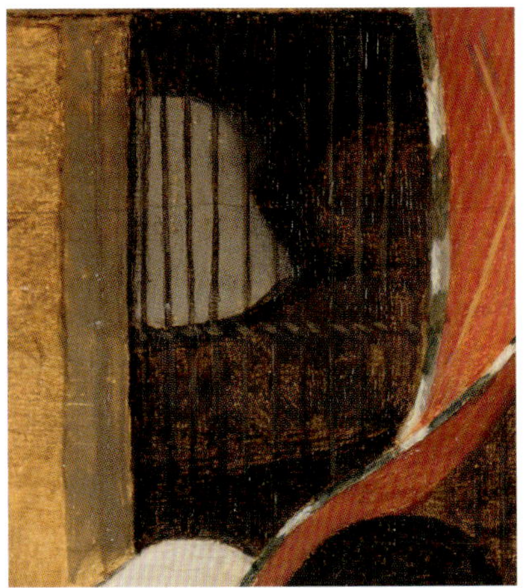

59. Detail of ill. pp. 18-19 © UGent, Gicas, 2018

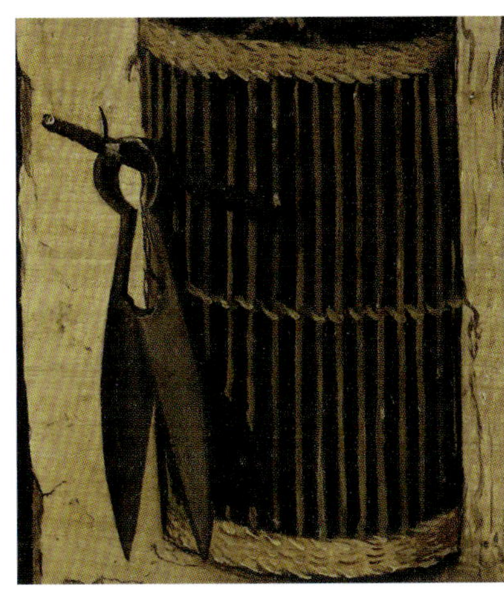

60. Detail of *NETHERLANDISH PROVERBS*
Berlin, Staatliche Museen Preussischer Kulturbesitz,
Gemäldegalerie © bpk-Bildagentur

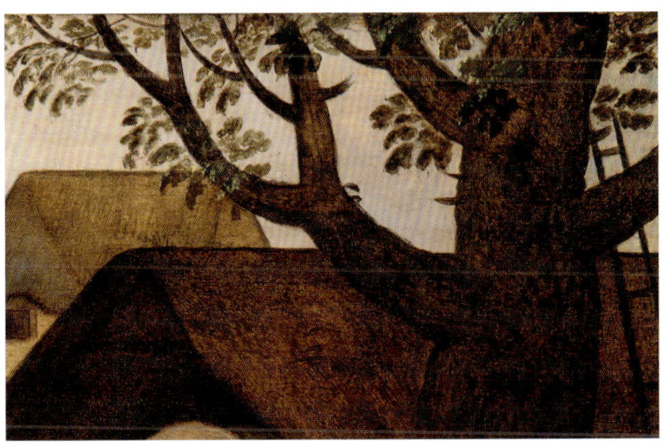

61. Detail of ill. pp. 18-19 © UGent, Gicas, 2018

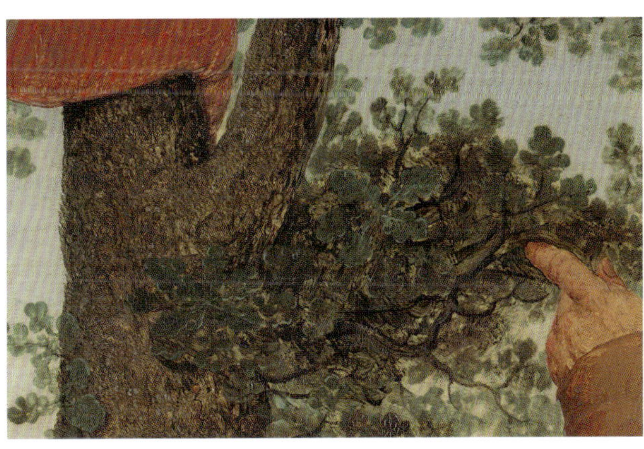

62. Detail of *THE BIRDNESTER*, Vienna, Kunsthistorisches Museum
© Vienna, Kunsthistorisches Museum

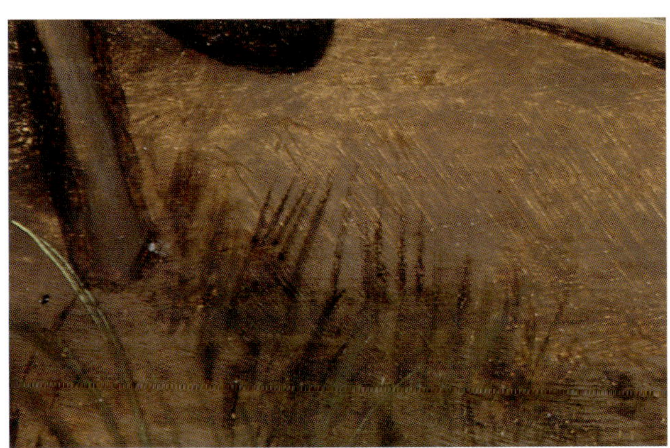

63. Detail of ill. pp. 18-19 © UGent, Gicas, 2018

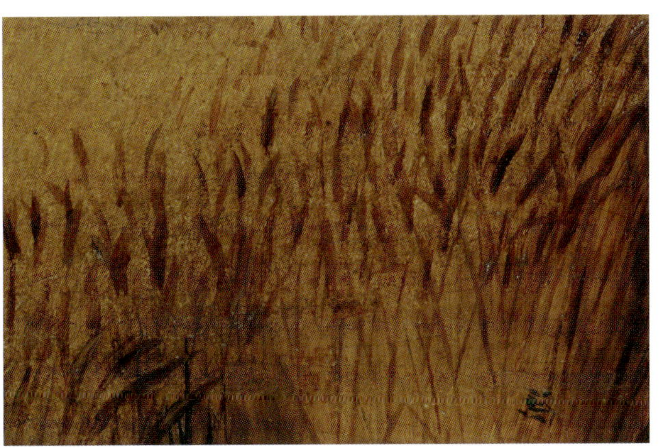

64. Detail of *THE HARVESTERS*, The Metropolitan Museum of Art
© The Metropolitan Museum of Art, New York

Like some other paintings in Pieter Bruegel the Elder's oeuvre, as e.g. the Rotterdam *Tower of Babel*, *Dancing Peasants at a St. Sebastian's Kermis* is not dated through an inscription. The observation that Bruegel's style is dependent on subject matter (and probably commission) rather than on stylistic development, makes dating our painting a rather difficult issue. Perhaps one characteristic in his oeuvre may unveil a clue. Pieter Bruegel is best known for large, complex multi-figured compositions with high horizon and an emphasis on encyclopedic detail, such as the Viennese *Childrens' Games*. However, now and then, he seems to have favored (or was commissioned) smaller, much more intimate and simple compositions. Among such early works, one can count the painted plates (*The Drunk Pushed in the Pigsty*, New York, private collection, 1557; and the *Twelve Proverbs*, Antwerp, Museum Mayer Van den Bergh, 1558) on the one hand, and the Berlin *Two Monkeys* (1562) on the other. Towards the middle and the end of his career, such smaller paintings seem to have appeared more frequently. The small grisailles, *The Death of the Virgin* (National Trust, Upton House) is situated around 1564 and *Christ and the Adulterous Woman* (London, Courtauld Institute)(1565). At the end of his career, the number of smaller formats increases: *Cocagne* (Munich, Alte Pinakothek)(1567), *The Birdnester* (Vienna, Kunsthistorisches Museum)(1568), *The Misanthrope* (Naples, Museo Nazionale di Capodimonte) (1568), *The Beggars* (Paris, Louvre, 1568), and the *Three Soldiers* in grisaille (New York, the Frick Collection)(1568).[45] Some of these paintings zoom in on motifs that appeared in earlier large format paintings. To us, it seems that *Dancing Peasants at a St. Sebastian's Kermis* follows this pattern: it is painted on a smaller format than employed usually by Bruegel, the composition is simplified, but based on a detail that appeared in his earlier drawing *Kermis at Hoboken* (London, Courtauld Institute) of 1559. For this reason, we are inclined to situate *Dancing Peasants at a St. Sebastian's Kermis* late in the artist's career, around 1567–1569.

Provenance and Attribution

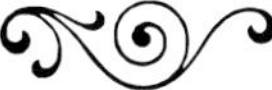

The painting surfaced first in public at the Brussels sale of the collection of Vicomte d'Angers (Brussels, 20 June 1925, lot 18),[46] where it was bought by the Berlin art gallery holder Paul Cassirer, who died a few months later (Görlitz, 1871 – Berlin, 1926). According to a note by Max J. Friedländer on the backside of a photograph in his archives (kept at The Hague, Rijksbureau voor Kunsthistorische Documentatie), the painting was auctioned at Sotheby's London on 7 June 1928 (lot 115), and was in the possession of a certain V.[on] Ruhemann in Berlin, May 1929, and possibly through the Berlin banker, Arthur Salomonsohn, sold to Heinrich Baron Thyssen-Bornemisza de Kászon (Mühlheim an der Ruhr, 1875 – Lugano, 1947) in August 1929 when it became part of his famous collection kept at his wife's family castle near the current Austrian-Hungarian border Rohonc (German: Reichnitz).[47] The following year, some masterpieces from this collection were shown to the public in an exhibition in the Neue Pinakothek in Munich.[48] During the 1930s, the collection was relocated to Villa Favorita at Castagnola near Lugano (Switzerland), where it was publically accessible between 1936 and 1939, and again after 1949. At his death in 1947, the painting was inherited by his second daughter, Gabrielle Baroness Bentinck-Thyssen-Bornemisza (Rohonc, 1915 – Paris, 1995). The baroness's collection kept in Paris, including the *Dancing Peasants at a St. Sebastian's Kermis*. Important works from the baroness's collection including our painting went on a world tour in 1986–1997.[49] The collection was auctioned at Sotheby's London on 6 December 1995 (lot 88), bought by an anonymous collector whom had it re-auctioned at the same house on 10 April 2003 (lot 10). It appeared last at auction, again at Sotheby's London on 7 December 2016 (lot 30), where the present owner acquired it.

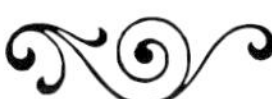

The painting was shown attributed to Pieter Bruegel the Elder in an exhibition held at the Neue Pinakothek in Munich in 1930, i.e. only a few months after its acquisition, devoted to the collection of Heinrich Baron Thyssen-Bornemisza, entitled *Sammlung Schloss Rohoncz*, (cat.no. 50). No doubt, Max Friedländer saw it there for the first time, acquired a black and white photograph of it and learned about its earlier provenance, which he, as mentioned above, noted carefully on its backside.[50] The great connoisseur published it in the first edition of his opus magnum *Die Altniederländische Malerei* (1937), in which he confirmed the attribution to Pieter Bruegel the Elder.[51] Also Edouard Michel (Paris, 1873–1953), curator at the Musée du Louvre, must have seen the work at the Munich exhibition, as he confirmed equally the attribution in his monograph devoted to Pieter Bruegel the Elder, which appeared only one year after the show.[52] With his attribution, Friedländer corrected Gustave Glück, director of the Kunsthistorisches Museum in Vienna until 1931 (Vienna, 1871 – Santa Monica, CA, 1952), who seems to be the only one at the time who considered it a work by Pieter Brueghel II.[53] Charles de Tolnay (Budapest, 1899 – Florence, 1981), in turn, thought the attribution was uncertain in his Bruegel monograph, published after he had fled Hamburg for Paris, where he worked as lecturer at the Institut d'art et d'archéologie of the Sorbonne.[54] Tolnay's monograph is considered now as more or less problematic where his attributions are concerned, as he was first and foremost a Michelangelo specialist.[55] In his 1937 catalogue of the Thyssen-Bornemisza collection, Heinemann adhered to the then nearly generally accepted attribution to Pieter the Elder.[56] Like Tolnay, Gotthard Jedlicka was again hesitant about the attribution in 1938.[57]

It is remarkable that *Dancing Peasants at a St. Sebastian's Kermis* received less attention in the art historical literature that appeared from about 1950s. There are three reasons for that: 1. Since 1947, it was no longer accessible to the public while in the collection of Baroness Bentinck-Thyssen; 2. It has undergone an unprofessional restoration, covering it with disfiguring overpaint and retouching; and last but not least, 3. Most authors had shifted their attention from connoisseurship to the iconographical meaning and cultural-historical place of Bruegel's oeuvre and concentrated therefore on the very famous works in large public museum collections. These are undoubtedly the reasons why Frits Grossmann, who was indeed interested in both historiography and iconography, did not mention the work in his 1955 monograph,[58] or that Philippe Roberts-Jones, the director of the Royal Museums of Fine Arts in Brussels, classified it under 'former attributions.'[59] Exceptions were the English edition of Friedländer's survey, *Early Netherlandish Painting*, where the former attribution was maintained,[60] and Valentin Denis (Leuven, 1916–1980), professor at the Catholic University Leuven, as Piero Bianconi (Minusio, 1899–1984), lecturer at the Bern University, both confirmed again Friedländer's attribution to Pieter Bruegel the Elder in their compilation books.[61]

In 1986–1987 the painting was shown again after many decades to the large public, attributed to Pieter Bruegel the Elder, in a travelling exhibition with a selection of Baroness's Bentick-Thyssen's collection with venues in Lausanne, Fondation de L'Hermitage; Paris, Musée Marmottan; Tokyo, Kumamoto-Toyama-Miyagi; Brussels, Palais des Beaux-Arts (where the present author saw it first), and Luxemburg, Musée de l'État.[62]

When the baroness's collection went up for auction after she had deceased, the condition of the painting was so deteriorated, that no one could recognize its original maker anymore. None of the recent authors have mentioned the painting in their studies on Pieter Bruegel the Elder anymore.[63] If they knew it, it was only from its lamentable state or from the bad black and white photograph in Friedländer.

Now *Dancing Peasants at a St. Sebastian's Kermis* has been cleaned and retouched, it has regained much of its original pictorial qualities through which it can be assessed much easier. As mentioned earlier, the painting is compositionally closely related to a figure group at the left side of Bruegel's drawing *Kermis at Hoboken* (London, Courtauld Institute). By zooming in on this group and placing the inn parallel to the picture plane, Bruegel arrived at a clear and easily legible composition, which fits the representational mode of some of his later, smaller paintings of the period c. 1567–1569.

The scientific analysis of the type of materials and the observations on how they were employed is in every respect characteristic of the manner of Pieter Bruegel the Elder. Oak quarterly split boards with typical slanting sides were butt joined with dowels. Subsequently, the panel was prepared with calcite ($CaCO_3$) mixed with animal glue. As is found in most paintings by Pieter Bruegel the Elder, the painting has an imprimatur consisting of a brownish ochre hue with some lead white and particles of carbon black mixed in.

The underdrawing is invisible to the naked eye, and even hard to distinguish through infrared reflectography. As in a large number of other Bruegel paintings, it has been traced, most probably from a 1:1 cartoon, and reinforced in a liquid material, likely to be identified as black carbonaceous ink. The underdrawing establishes most contours in figuration, architecture and other compositional elements. Finally, the pigments that have been identified fits the palette encountered in other paintings by Bruegel.

Although it could be argued that most of these materials are also encountered in other Flemish paintings of the second half of the 16th century, their specific usage is idiosyncratic. The construction of a panel with slanting boards is very particular, as is the employment of a 1:1 cartoon to transfer an invention to its final wooden support. Thus far, these specifics have been observed only in Pieter Bruegel the Elder's paintings.

Evidently, this holds equally for the particular handling of paint, which can be characterized as economic, quick and '*alla prima*'. In the final result, the vibrating imprimatura plays a fundamental role and the patchy dabbed zones with much tonal differentiation is nothing less than a personal signature painting technique of Bruegel. In comparison to the way most of his contemporaries worked, we have coined his technique with a modern term '*avant garde*'.

Most of Bruegel's figures — male, female as well as children —, often with round caricature-like faces and prominent features are easily recognizable types that are encountered in all of his paintings. Also figures seen from the back, which draw the observer's gaze into the composition, are so characteristic that they can be considered without hesitation as Bruegel hallmarks. The convincing suggestion of movement and swaying elegance of those coarse peasants is so proper to Pieter Bruegel the Elder's hand that none of his copyists was able to imitate. *Dancing Peasants at a St. Sebastian's Kermis* offers a wealth of peasants' clothing and other elements of material culture, painted exactly in the very same way as encountered in his other paintings.

In conclusion, after it first surfaced in public, *Dancing Peasants at a St. Sebastian's Kermis* was recognized as a work by Pieter Bruegel the Elder, among others by Max Friedländer, the great connoisseur of Flemish painting. However, after it entered the collection of Baroness Bentinck-Thyssen-Bornemisza, the scholarly interest in the painting diminished. When it reappeared many decades later on the art market in a heavily restored condition, its artistic qualities could no longer be appreciated. Only after a recent judicious conservation treatment, a scientific examination of its materials and a new evaluation of its painting technique and style, the painting can be returned to one of the greatest masters of Western art history, Pieter Bruegel the Elder.

Endnotes

[1] The term 'enterprise' is taken from Maastricht / Brussels 2001.
[2] Lichtert 2015.
[3] Van Mander (ed.Miedema) 1994-1997.
[4] As can be seen in a painting with the same theme, attributed to Pieter Balten, see https://rkd.nl/nl/explore/images/record?query=kermis&start=248
[5] Sellink & Silva Maroto 2011
[6] Sellink 2011, 132, no. 78.
[7] *Ordonnancien Ende Decreten, Vanden Heylighen Concilie Generael Ghehouden Tot Trenten*, Antwerp 1565, 244-245, cited by Sellink & Silva Maroto 2011, 791, n. 40.
8 P. Bloccius & J. Pieters, *Meer Dan Twee Hondert Ketteryen, Blasphemien Vvelck Vvt De Misse Zyn Ghecomen* (…), Wesel 1567, 72-73, also cited in Ibid.
[9] Sellink 2011, 126-128.
[10] Bruegel's drawing of Hoboken kermis became the example for many followers, among whom Jacob Savery (°Courtrai, 1566 - †Amsterdam, 1603)(see e.g. hand colored drawing in London, Victoria and Albert Museum).
[11] Van Mander (ed.Miedema) 1994-1997, I, 190.
[12] Quoted by Silver 2012, 103.
[13] Sellink & Silva Maroto 2011.
[14] Another anonymous copy, formerly in the collection of the Berlin art dealer Paul Cassirer († 1926), London, mentioned in the literature perhaps is perhaps identical with this one (Michel 1931) (otherwise whereabouts unknown). Equally mentioned in the literature is an anonymous partial reduced copy, formerly in the Mrs Dr Salomonsohn collection, Berlin, and later in the Delaroff Gallery in St Petersburg, depicts only the tavern door on the right of the composition (Friedländer 1937, 111 and Michel 1931, 80).
[15] On Bruegel's compositional strategies, see Sellinck in Vienna 2018, 295 ff (e-book)
[16] See e.g. https://rkd.nl/explore/images/57633. Ertz 2000, vol. II, 883-891, cat.nrs 1296-1332.
[17] See https://rkd.nl/explore/images/29834
[18] https://rkd.nl/explore/images/61991. This drawing was the design of a print by Nicolaes de Bruyn of 1603, which was used for paintings, among others by Bartholomeus Grondonck in 1617, see https://rkd.nl/explore/images/20524.
[19] Many crucial works by Bruegel have been examined in the context of the Bruegel exhibition, which opened in Vienna, Oct. 2018. Before that, only a few detailed technical reports on Bruegel paintings had been published: those on the *Census in Bethlehem* (Brussels, KMSKB-MRBAB), *the Sermon of St John* (Budapest, Szépmüvészeti Múzeum), *Winter Landscape with Bird Trap* (Brussels, KMSKB-MRBAB), and *The Adoration of the Magi* (Winterthur, Dr Oskar Reinhardt Collection "Am Römerholz") (all by Currie & Allart 2012), and *Mad Meg* (a.k.a. *Dulle Griet*, Antwerp, Mayer Van den Bergh Museum)(Martens 2012; Van de Voorde et al. 2014). In Currie & Allart 2012, other paintings that have been (partly) technically examined are mentioned. During the preparation of the Bruegel exhibition at the Kunsthistorisches Museum, Vienna, the Bruegel paintings in this collection have been technically investigated; see Vienna 2018.
[20] All imaging techniques were performed by Ghent interdisciplinary Centre for Art and Science, the research group headed by the author (Ghent University, Belgium). X-ray imaging was performed by Dr. med. F. Cuigniez (Ghent, Belgium).
[21] All chemical analyses were undertaken by Raman Spectroscopy Research Group, headed by Prof. dr. Peter Vandenabeele (Ghent University, Belgium)
[22] Wood is a hygroscopic and anisotropic material, which implies that it is susceptible to shrinking and expanding due to fluctuations in relative temperature and humidity on the one hand, as well as to wrapping due to its different mechanical properties in its three structural directions.
[23] Streeton & Wadum 2012.
[24] Wadum 1998. In the Viennese Bruegel paintings, the width of full planks varies between 22 and 34 cm; see Oberhaler in Vienna 2018, 374.
[25] Klein 2012.
[26] Oberthaler in Vienna 2018, 370-373 (e-book).
[27] Currie & Allart, I, 245. The presence of the cradle seriously hampers the legibility of the XR-image.
[28] Verougstraete-Marcq 1985, 21-27; Van Hout 1998, 199-225; Van Hout & Balis 2010, 42-51; Martens 2012, 59, n. 12.
[29] Currie & Allart 2012, I, 251.
[30] A very similar hue has been found in *Dulle Griet*; see Martens 2012, 33. The same imprimatura was found also in the Viennese Bruegel paintings, with the exception of the Seasons panels and the late *Peasant Wedding* and *Peasant Kermis*; see Oberthaler in Vienna 2018, 375 (e-book).
[31] It is less likely that lead white was mixed in the ground at that time, see Stols-Witlox 2012.
[32] In order to compare the painted stage with the underdrawing, both the IRR and VIS documents were scaled to the same pixel size and resolution, and subsequently layered in Photoshop CC 2018®. The layers were not registered by dedicated software, and differences in optical aberration of the lenses used in different modalities could not be neutralized. Moreover, the cartoon may have shifted slightly during the transferal process. For these reasons, every detail could only be studied after repositioning the VIS layer on the IRR one, based on reference points.
[33] Similar changes in positions of heads can be observed in *The Drunk Pushed in the Pigsty* (New York, private collection) and in the head of Christ in *Christ carrying the Cross* (Vienna, Kunsthistorisches Museum); see Van Schoute & Verougstraete 2000 and Pénot & Oberthaler in Vienna 2018, 197.
[34] Martens 2012.
[35] Currie & Allart 2012, I, 262.
[36] Oberthaler in Vienna 2018, 380-398 (e-book). Oberthaler

assumes rightfully that Bruegel adapted his underdrawing style to the subject matter of his paintings (Ibid., 380).

[37] Currie & Allart 2012, I, 116; 262.

[38] Spronk in Vienna 2018, 365 (e-book).

[39] Based on the analysis of the Viennese paintings, Oberthaler characterized Bruegel's palette as follows: "The pigments employed by Bruegel are not uncommon but are typical of the period and region. These are earth pigments (red and yellow ochres, umber), lead-tin yellow, vermilion, bone black, plant black and, of course, lead white. Green is commonly created through the mixture of azurite and lead-tin yellow, as in the green landscapes of *The Tower of Babel* and *The Birdnester.* Azurite was the preferred blue pigment, found particularly in many sky passages. However, several skies also contain the cooler pigment smalt"; see Oberthaler in Vienna 2018, 401. This description matches perfectly the pigments found in the *Dancing Peasants at St. Sebastian's Kermis*.

[40] Organic pigments cannot be identified by XRF due to their low atomic weight and often not by raman.

[41] In *Dulle Griet* many of the same pigments have been identified, except smalt, the reds are only vermillion (HgS), while the green areas consist often of discolored copper resinate; see Van de Voorde, et al. 2014. Bruegel sometimes used azurite and smalt in the same painting, e.g. in the sky of *The Conversion of Saul*; see Pénot & Oberthaler in Vienna 2018, p. 249.

[42] Friedländer 1976, 45, no. 33, pl. 41.

[43] Van Mander (ed.Miedema) 1994-1997, I, 190.

[44] Oberthaler in Vienna 2018, 401 (e-book).

[45] Sellink discusses the late 'tonal' paintings in Vienna 2018, 285.

[46] Very little can be found on this aristocratic family. A Vicomte d'Angers was mayor of the French village La Chapelle-Viel in the department de L'Orne in 1856. (Conseil general du department du Calvados, *Session de 1856. Rapport du Préfet et deliberations du conseil*, Caen: Pagny, 1856). Maybe the painting formed part of the collection sold by a later descendant of the family, perhaps his son or grandson in Brussels in 1925.

[47] On Heinrich Baron Thyssen-Bornemisza see the English and German Wikipediae websites, that unfortunately contain contradicting information: https://en.wikipedia.org/wiki/Heinrich_Thyssen and https://de.wikipedia.org/wiki/Heinrich_Thyssen.

[48] Munich 1930, no. 50.

[49] Lausanne et al. 1986-87, no. 8.

[50] This inscription reads 'Sotheby / P. Cassirer / V.[on] Ruhemann / V.1929 / Attest / cf. Salomonsohn, / Berlin / B / Thyssen / VIII. 29'.

[51] Friedländer 1937, 60, no. 32.

[52] Michel 1931, 80.

[53] Glück 1931, no. 73. He repeated this opinion in his second book, Glück 1951, no. 88.

[54] Tolnay 1935, 97, no. 60.

[55] For Tolnay, see L. Sorensen, ed. "Charles de Tolnay" In Dictionary of Art Historians. Retrieved August 06, 2018, Web site: http://www.arthistorians.info/tolnayc

[56] Heinemann 1937, vol. I, no. 62.

[57] Jedlicka 1938, 540.

[58] Grossmann 1955.

[59] Roberts-Jones 1969, 99, and again in his upadted edition, Roberts-Jones 1997, 328.

[60] Friedländer 1976, 45, no. 33, pl. 41.

[61] Denis 1952, 34; Bianconi 1969, 105, no. 43 (datable to '1565?').

[62] *La Collection Bentinck-Thyssen*, 1986–87, no. 8.

[63] It is not mentioned by Marijnissen & Ruyffelaere 1988, Sellink 2006, nor Silver 2011. The only one who still commented on it was Klaus Ertz in his monograph on Pieter Brueghel the Younger, reacting against Glück, that it was certainly not a work by the son (Ertz 2000, I, 289, vol. II, 913, cat. no. A1277).

Literature

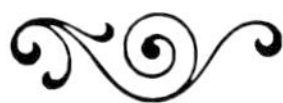

Bianconi 1969:
P. Bianconi, *The Complete Paintings of Bruegel* (Milan, 1969), 105, no. 43 (*as Pieter Bruegel the Elder, and datable to '1565?').

Currie & Allart 2012:
C. Currie, & D. Allart, *The Brueg(H)el Phenomenon: Paintings by Pieter Bruegel the Elder and Pieter Brueghel the Younger with a Special Focus on Technique and Copying Practice*, 3 vols. (Turnhout: Brepols, 2012).

Denis 1952:
V. Denis, *Tutta la pittura di Pieter Bruegel* (Milan, 1952), 34 (*as Pieter Bruegel the Elder).

Ertz 2000:
K. Ertz, *Pieter Brueghel der Jüngere* (Lingen, 2000), vol. I, p. 289, vol. II, 913, cat. no. A1277 (*as not by Pieter Brueghel the Younger).

Friedländer 1937:
M. J. Friedländer, *Die Altniederländische Malerei*, vol. XIV (Leiden, 1937), 60, no. 32 (*as Pieter Bruegel the Elder).

Friedländer 1976:
M.J. Friedländer, *Early Netherlandish Painting*, vol. XIV (Leiden and Brussels, 1976), 45, no. 33, reproduced pl. 41 (*as Pieter Bruegel the Elder).

Glück 1931:
G. Glück, *Brueghels Gemälde* (Vienna, 1931), no. 73 (*as Pieter Brueghel the Younger).

Glück 1951:
G. Glück, *Das Grosse Bruegel-Werk* (Vienna 1951), no. 88 (*as Brueghel the Younger).

Grossmann 1955:
F. Grossmann, Fritz, *Bruegel: The Paintings: Complete Edition* (London: Phaidon press, 1955).

Heinemann 1937:
R. Heinemann, *Sammlung Schloss Rohoncz* (Zurich, 1937), vol. I, no. 62 (*as Pieter Bruegel the Elder).

Jedlicka 1938:
G. Jedlicka, *Pieter Bruegel, Der Maler in seiner Zeit* (Zurich, 1938), 540 (*as attribution doubtful).

Klein 2012:
P. Klein, "Wood identification and dendrochronology", in J. Hill Stoner & R. Rushfield (eds.), *Conservation of Easel Paintings* (London & New York: Routledge, 2012), 51–65.

Lausanne et al. 1986-87:
Lausanne, Fondation de L'Hermitage; Paris, Musée Marmottan; Tokyo, Kumamoto-Toyama-Miyagi; Brussels, Palais des Beaux-Arts; Luxembourg, Musée de l'État, *La Collection Bentinck-Thyssen*, 1986–1987, no. 8 (*as Pieter Bruegel the Elder).

Lichtert 2015:
K. Lichtert, 'New Perspectives on Pieter Bruegel the Elder's Journey to Italy (c. 1552-1554/1555),' *Oud Holland* 128 (1), 39–54.

Maastricht / Brussels 2001:
P. van den Brink (ed.), *Brueghel Enterprises*, cat. exh. Maastricht, Bonnefantenmuseum / Brussels, Musées Royaux des Beaux-Arts de Belgique, Brussels, March 22 – June 23, 2000–2002 (Amsterdam/Ghent: Ludion, 2001).

Marijnissen & Ruyffelaere 1988:
R.H. Marijnissen & P. Ruyffelaere, *Bruegel: Het Volledig Oeuvre* (Antwerpen: Mercatorfonds, 1988).

Martens 2012:
M. Martens, 'Het realisatieproces in *Dulle Griet* en de *Twaalf Spreuken* van Pieter Bruegel de Oude', in *Pieter Bruegel Ongezien! De verborgen Antwerpse collecties*, ed. M. Sellink, M.P.J. Martens, Museum Mayer van den Bergh, Antwerp (Leuven: Davidsfonds, 2012), 26–59.

Michel 1931:
E. Michel (ed.), *Bruegel* (Paris 1931), 80 (*as Pieter Bruegel the Elder)

Roberts-Jones 1969:
P. Roberts-Jones et al., *Bruegel: the Painter and his world*, 1969, 99 (*under former attributions)

Munich 1930:
Munich, Neue Pinakothek, *Sammlung Schloss Rohoncz*, 1930, no. 50 (*as by Pieter Bruegel the Elder)

Roberts-Jones 1997:
P. & F. Roberts-Jones, *Pierre Bruegel l'Ancien* (Paris 1997), 328 (*under 'Attributions anciennes ou récentes').

Sellink & Silva Maroto 2011:
M. Sellink & P. Silva Maroto, 'The Rediscovery of Pieter Bruegel the Elder's "Wine of St Martin's Day", Acquired for the Museo Nacional Del Prado, Madrid,' *Burlington Magazine* 153 (1305): 784–793.

Sellink 2011:
M. Sellink, *Bruegel: The Complete Paintings, Drawings and Prints* (Antwerp: Ludion 2011).

Silver 2012:
L. Silver, *Peasant Scenes and Landscapes: The Rise of Pictorial Genres in the Antwerp Art Market* (Philadelphia: University of Pennsylvania Press, 2012).

Streeton & Wadum, 2012:
N. Streeton, J. Wadum, 'Northern European panel paintings,' in J. Hill Stoner & R. Rushfield (eds.), *Conservation of Easel Paintings* (London & New York: Routledge, 2012), 86–97.

Tolnay 1935:
C. de Tolnay, *Pierre Bruegel l'Ancien* (Brussels 1935), 97, no. 60 (*as attribution uncertain)

Van de Voorde et al. 2014:
L. Van de Voorde, J. Van Pevenage, K. De Langhe, M.P.J. Martens, et al., 'Non-destructive in Situ Study of "Mad Meg" by Pieter Bruegel the Elder Using Mobile X-ray Fluorescence, X-ray Diffraction and Raman Spectrometers,' *Spectrochimica Acta Part A- Atomic spectroscopy*, 97 (2014), 1–6.

Van Hout & Balis 2010:
N. Van Hout & A. Balis, *Rubens doorgelicht. Meekijken over de schouder van een virtuoos* (Antwerp: Ludion, 2010).

Van Hout 1998:
N. Van Hout, 'Meaning and Development of the Ground Layer in Seventeenth Century Painting,' in E. Hermens, A. Ouwerkerk & N. Costaras (eds.), *Looking through Paintings, Leids Kunsthistorisch Jaarboek*, 11 (1998), 199–225.

Van Mander (ed. Miedema) 1994–1997:
Karel van Mander, *The lives of the illustrious Netherlandish and German painters, from the first edition of the Schilder-boeck (1603-1604), preceded by the lineage, circumstances and place of birth, life and..., from the second edition of the Schilder-boeck (1616-1618)*, 6 vols. (Soest: Davaco, 1994–1997).

Van Schoute & Verougstraete 2000:
R. van Schoute & H. Verougstraete, 'A painted wooden roundel by Pieter Bruegel the Elder', *The Burlington Magazine*, CXLII (March 2000), 140–146.

Verougstraete-Marcq 1985:
H. Verougstraete-Marcq, 'L'imprimatura et la manière striée. Quelques exemples dans la peinture flamande du 15e au 17e siècle,' in H. Verougstraete & R. Van Schoute (eds.), *Le dessin sous-jacent dans la Peinture. Colloque VI: Infrarouge et autres techniques d'examen* (Louvain-la-Neuve, 1985), 21–27.

Vienna 2018:
E. Oberthaler, S. Pénot, M. Sellink & R. Spronk, Bruegel, *Bruegel*, cat. exh. (Vienna: Kunsthistorisches Museum, 2018).

Wadum 1998:
J. Wadum, *Historical Overview of Panel-Making Techniques in the Northern Countries*, in K. Dardes & A. Rohe (eds.), *The Structural Conservation of Panel Paintings: Proceedings of a Symposium at the J. Paul Getty Museum, April 1995* (Los Angeles: Getty Conservation Institute, 1998), 149–177.

* Mentions explicitly the *Dancing Peasants at a St. Sebastian Kermis*

简介

2016年，我们在一层层粗糙的修复和后来刷上的旧颜料下面，幸运地认出了一副被早期佛兰德绘画的鉴赏大师麦克斯·弗里德兰德（1867年生于柏林，1958年死于阿姆斯特丹）认定为老彼得·勃鲁盖尔（1525-1569年，布鲁塞尔）所画的作品。技术鉴定和谨慎的清洁向我们揭示了多种带有大师特征的绘画风格和技巧。这些多元化的证据让我们不得不重新审视这幅画作，将《圣塞巴斯蒂安市集上跳舞的农民》回归它的原创者，与老彼得·勃鲁盖尔的其他杰作并驾齐驱（Ill. XXX）。我们会在扩展视野的同时讨论这幅画在十六世纪北欧文化中的历史地位。

老彼得·勃鲁盖尔，也被称作‘彼得·勃鲁盖尔一世’，早在1569年去世后就很快赢得了声誉。让人惊叹的是，那时他的大部分画作已经被欧洲最尊贵的皇室收藏，是上流社会收藏家们极力追捧的艺术品。比如红衣主教格兰维尔，哈尔斯堡王朝重要的政治家，就被告知这些画作要成堆的金钱才能买到。事实上，勃鲁格尔的真迹在艺术品市场上十分稀少。他的长子彼得二世（1564年生于布鲁塞尔，1638年死于安特卫普）成功地建立了商业化的合作关系来填补这个巨大的空缺，通过其他画家仿制了许多他父亲的作品。

关于勃鲁盖尔的史料保存下来的很少，使我们对他的一生知之甚少。这与他显赫的盛名造成了鲜明的对比。在去世后不久，他的出生日期和地点就成为争议的话题。我们并不确切知道他是在哪里，跟随哪一位艺术家，受到了绘画，制图和平面设计的训练。虽然我们对他参与的社会关系网络有一些认识，但是对他艺术知识的构成以及交往的人群，我们几乎不得而知。幸运的是，勃鲁盖尔留下的艺术作品向我们清晰地展示了他作为一位博学和几乎肯定是带有批评性的艺术家的地位——一位博学的画家。

有关勃鲁盖尔生平的信息如此之少，并不只是一件让二十一世纪艺术史家烦恼的事。对一个从有生之年开始，直到现在都被大众仰慕，被公认为西方欧洲艺术最重要的艺术家之一的画家来说，这是一件让人惊叹的事。可是对我们来说，这也是一个挑战，要将他留下的作品充分地运用为考证历史的依据。幸运的是，大部分的画作他都签了名字和日期，使我们能够重新组建他在艺术上的发展过程。更进一步来说，他在艺术界同行中的声誉留下了深远的艺术影响，这也是一个重要的信息来源。总的来说，这些就是我们能够用来重建勃鲁盖尔生平与作品的基本构件。

勃鲁格尔的绘画，素描和印刷品展现了他非凡的复杂性。他最优秀的作品是在欧洲最动荡的历史时期内完成的。那是一个宗教，社会和政治都充满了冲突的时期。这些历史环境，再加上对他的生平缺乏确凿的信息，使对他作品的评价意见不一。

勃鲁格尔曾经被认作‘第二个耶罗尼米斯·博斯’，一个对大快朵颐的农民的行为超乎寻常地着迷的幽默家。在十九世纪，他因此经常被称作是‘农民勃鲁格尔’，以便与他的儿子‘苦不堪言’彼得二世和‘天鹅绒’扬一世区分。对其他人来说，他其实更是一个埃拉斯姆哲学思想兴起时期学识渊博的人道主义者。从二十世纪六十年代开始，评论对他在社会中的地位从批判天主教压制审判转换到了对新兴资本主义的抗议，而同时其他作者仍然将他看作一个参与炼金术和玄学的异教徒。虽然有关勃鲁格尔的专门文献充斥着各种没有根据的臆想，这种显然充满冲突和对立的解释并不是对他的研究所独有的。形式，内容和功能上的复杂性是十六世纪北欧社会最根本的普遍性质，而勃鲁格尔是那个社会最出色的艺术代言人。

在最近的几十年中，专家们尽了长足的努力，将虚构从真实的历史中剔除。绘画和素描从勃鲁格尔核心的杰作中被撤了出来。但是幸运的是，随着新的科学技术和证据产生，一副珍贵的，也许从未被发现，也许几乎被忘却的作品重新浮现，给了我们探寻根源的可能性。

Maximiliaan Martens教授
根特大学——比利时皇家佛兰德科学与艺术学院
2018年7月

生平

直到1563年，老彼得·勃鲁格尔　都是主要在安特卫普工作。那里是早期现代西欧北部最大的商业都市之一。就像这座欣欣向荣的城市里许多艺术家一样，他也是来自荷兰其他城市的移民，被到处是合适顾客的机会而吸引。他的出生地不详，但是像许多移民一样，他的名字被认为是地名字源，也就是说源自他的故乡的名字。曾经有学者试图溯源到勃鲁格尔，现在的松和步勒郝尔镇（位于现属荷兰的北布拉班特省的埃因霍恩北部）的一支。最早的佛兰德绘画史家卡莱尔·范·曼德（1548年生于莫莱贝克，1606年死于阿姆斯特丹）将他的出生地写为布洛格尔。这可能是指马赛克附近的格罗特·布洛格尔，现属比利时林佩省。在十六世纪的历史记载中这里经常被称作‘勃鲁格尔’。或是指靠近‘克林布洛格尔’。但是，仅仅在勃鲁格尔去世前两年，落多维科·圭恰蒂尼（1521年生于佛罗伦萨，1589年死于安特卫普），一个住在安特卫普的来自佛罗伦萨的商人，首次提到了画家的出生地。在他《对低地国的描述》（1567年）中，圭恰蒂尼记载画家的出生地为布利达，布拉班特省的主要城市之一。布利达大约在安特卫普东北方向五十公里。它与其他小一些的村镇不同，是当时的艺术中心。与彼得同时期的肖像画家威廉·奇（约1515年生于布利达，1568年死于安特卫普）也是来自布利达。迄今为止，这个画家生平中的谜团仍未解决。

同样不得而知的是彼得出生的日期以及关于他的教育和早期艺术生涯的直接信息。1551年，他成为圣卢克安特卫普画家协会中的一名独立大师。从统计来看，大部分人是在成年期（当时为25岁）获得这个称呼的。如果勃鲁格尔也属于这种情况的话，他可能是在1526年左右出生的。他的名字第一次被记载是在1550-1551年。作为几乎与他完全同时期的彼得·巴尔腾（安特卫普1525-1584年）的工作室助理，为梅赫伦手套制作行业商会创作单幅祭坛画。范·曼德接下来告诉我们，勃鲁格尔在出名的画家，设计师彼得·库克·范·阿尔斯特（1502年生于阿尔斯特，1550年死于布鲁塞尔）工作室实习。除了作师傅，彼得·库克的女儿梅坎于1563年嫁给勃鲁格尔，他也成了丈人。这个生活经历也许可以解释为什么在库克作为工作室主管去世以后，勃鲁格尔立即获得了独立大师资格。不管怎样，合作者在师傅去世后自立门户，甚至接管生意，是一件寻常的事情。在他的师傅和丈人扬·马丁·范·多尼克（1470年生于图而奈，1527年死于安特卫普）去世后，彼得·库克在1527年做了完全同样的事。让人惊叹的是，彼得·勃鲁格尔的早期作品完全没有被认为是他师傅的彼得·库克的风格。这也许可以被理解为勃鲁格尔在艺术生涯的非常早期就发展了自己的风格，或者是库克的风格到了1550年已经不再时兴。

虽然我们对老彼得·勃鲁格尔的早期生涯几乎一无所知，我们对1552年以后发生的事还是有所了解。就在成为独立大师以后，他开始了几乎耗时两年的行程，去了意大利。最近一个以他署名的素描为依据的研究重建了他的旅行——从普罗旺斯，到地中海海岸，到罗马，继续南行到西西里，然后经阿尔卑斯返回[1]。勃鲁格尔对古典文化的反响还是很有限的，他的两个版本的巴别塔（藏于鹿特丹，勃曼斯美术馆和维也纳，艺术史博物馆）显然受到了罗马斗兽场的启发。他对更近期的意大利艺术的兴趣也一样是不冷不热，虽然如果没有波提切利的样本，他的素描《阿佩莱瑟的诽谤》（藏于伦敦，大英博物馆）简直无法想象。

与此相反，阿尔卑斯山的宏伟给我们的艺术家留下了深刻的印象。范·曼德生动地描绘了这一印象，好像‘他吞下了这些山与石，然后回到家将它们吐到了画布和画幅上’[2]。罗耶尼米斯·考克（安特卫普1518-1570年）的印刷工作间‘四阵风’　将部分素描以印刷品出版。在1553年从意大利回来以后，勃鲁格尔继续为考克设计印刷品。直到1557年他第一幅有时间记录的画面世，这好像是他的主要工作。范·曼德同时向我们揭示了勃鲁格尔的性格。他形容这位艺术家沉静，但是开朗。他渐渐受到波西的启发，因此被人称作‘大粪彼得’。他的作品给观赏者带来了笑容。与他的亲密朋友，商人汉斯·佛兰科特一起，他愉快地参加了农民的集市和婚礼。在这些场合，他们穿着和农民一样的服装，农民的习俗和举止给他们带来了无尽的快乐。

在1563年与梅坎·库克结婚后，这对年轻夫妻移居到了布利塞尔。还是范·曼德为此事件提供了更多信息。看来是他的丈母，彼得·库克的遗孀，梅坎·佛赫斯特坚持他们搬家的。她想借此阻止彼得与另一个女人交往。

仅仅六年以后，老彼得·勃鲁格尔于1569年9月9日去世，葬于布鲁塞尔中心的小堂教堂。范·曼德知道他在垂死之际让妻子毁掉了一些素描，以免为她招来麻烦。这一要求尤其引来了对勃鲁格尔激进的政治观点的种种猜测。他死后除了遗孀外还留下了两个幼年的儿子，彼得二世（1564年生于布鲁塞尔，1638年死于安特卫普）和扬一世（1568年生于布鲁塞尔，1625年死于安特卫普）。据范·曼德记载，扬在祖母梅坎·佛赫斯特的调教下成为画家。新的一代将他们的名字写为勃鲁格尔（Brueghel，加上h），老彼得后来也在1559年以后用这种拼写法改名为勃鲁格尔（Bruegel，没有h）。如前面所提到，彼得·勃鲁格尔二世继续通过制作大量复制品来推广他父亲的原创画作。但是与他的兄弟比起来才华横溢的扬·勃鲁格尔一世，最终成为有创意的艺术家。他受到高度的赞扬，并与同时期出名的艺术家，比如彼得保罗·鲁本斯·合作。

在勃鲁格尔去世之后仅仅三年，多米尼克·兰索尼斯（1536年左右生于布吕赫，1599年死于列日）将他包括在自己的《艺术家肖像和绘画集》（1572年出版）中。这部带有蚀刻肖像的二十三位著名荷兰艺术家的颂歌显然包括了老彼得·勃鲁格尔（最初被称为是‘新波西’，兰索尼斯在第二版（编于1600年）对勃鲁格尔的欣赏转变为将他称为那个时代最重要的艺术家。）我们并不知道兰索尼斯是否与彼得·勃鲁格尔见过面。不过，著名的绘图家，地理家和人道主义者，亚伯拉罕·奥特留斯（安特卫普1527-1598年）却与画家私交甚密，甚至拥有他所作的《处女之死》（现藏阿普顿庄园，班博理，英国名胜古迹托管协会）。除了因出版第一部现代地图册《世界之舞台》（1570年）而著名，奥特留斯还在1573年出版了《签名集》，在书中对自己才华横溢的朋友的早逝不胜悲哀。与兰索尼斯一样，奥特留斯称勃鲁格尔‘毫无疑问是他那个时代最重要的画家’，赞扬了他对绘画主题自然主义的表现手法。自然是他唯一的模特，他甚至‘画了很多不能画的东西，给大家更多的思考，而不是更多的观察’。还有我们关于勃鲁格尔生平最丰富的信息来源（并非总是值得信赖）——卡莱尔·范·曼德——也在《画家之书》中称赞了他对自然的模仿。这一技巧是他特别在意大利的巡游中掌握的。

勃鲁格尔也可能有反对者，因为他的创作既不合乎佛兰德的艺术传统，也不把他同时期艺术家的‘浪漫主义’艺术理想化。来自根特的修辞学家卢卡斯·德赫利（根特1534-1584年）不仅是扬·范·艾科众多狂热追随者中的一个，也是他的老师佛朗斯·佛劳里斯（安特卫普1519/20-1570年）的崇拜者。他毫无疑问是十六世纪安特卫普画家中与勃鲁格尔在艺术上绝对相对立的人。在他最著名的著作《诗歌的花园与果园》（1565年）中，他谴责地写到‘某一位画家，侮辱了安特卫普的所有画家’。‘某人曾去罗马，但是在他那些上不了台面的帆布画布上画的，比胆汁还要苦的画里，找不到一丁点古代或是现代的伟大的意大利大师的痕迹。’据许多专家的考证，这个‘某人’，就是经常用帆布画布的彼得·勃鲁格尔。也许，德赫利的文字反映出一个艺术原理上的争论——佛劳里斯传统的，画工精美，高高在上的‘浪漫主义’艺术，与老彼得·勃鲁格尔前卫的，粗糙的，简洁描绘的农民场景的争论。佛劳里斯的作品满是激起关于经典的古典主义知识思考的寓言，而勃鲁格尔的画是对当代生活直接的抨击和道德寓言。不过，毫无疑问两者都是以城市精英社会阶层为主要对象的。

归因

这幅画于1930年在慕尼黑的新绘画陈列馆展出时是以老彼得·勃鲁格尔署名。仅仅在被收藏几个月以后，在这个名为‘落宏兹城堡藏品’的展览中展出，它属于海因里奇男爵提森-博内米萨收藏品中的一副 （编号50）。毫无疑问，麦克斯·弗里德兰德在那里第一次见到了这幅画。他获得了一张画的黑白照片，开始研究它的早期出处，并将结果仔细地在照片背面记录下来[3]。这位伟大的鉴赏家第一次在他的巨作《早期尼德兰绘画》（1937年）中提到这幅画，并确认为老彼得·勃鲁格尔所作[4]。同时卢浮宫的馆长爱德华德·米切尔（巴黎1873-1953年）也一定是在慕尼黑展览上见到了这幅画。他同样在自己一年后发表的关于老彼得·勃鲁格尔的专著中，将它归在勃鲁格尔名下[5]。有了这个来源上的肯定，弗里德兰德纠正了古斯塔夫·格鲁克（1871年生于维也纳，1952年死于加州圣莫妮卡）的说法。格鲁克到1931年为止是维也纳艺术史博物馆的馆长，当时只有他一个人认为这幅画是彼得·勃鲁格尔二世所作[6]。查理·德·托尔尼（1899年生于布达佩斯特，1981年死于弗洛伦萨）在从汉堡逃离到巴黎后，在索邦的艺术与考古研究所讲课。他在巴黎出版了关于勃鲁格尔德专著，认为这幅画的作者不能肯定[7]。托尔尼的专著中关于来源的探讨现在被认为是有些问题的，因为他首先是一个米开朗琪罗的专家[8]。在他1937年出版的提森-博内米萨收藏目录中，海尼曼采用了当时几乎普遍接受的观点，将画作归在老彼得·勃鲁格尔名下[9]。与托尔尼一样，格萨德·杰立卡在1938年再次对画的作者提出质疑[10]。

《圣塞巴斯蒂安市集上跳舞的农民》在大约1950年代以后的艺术史出版物上受到了较少关注，这是一件让人惊叹的事。这里面有三个原因：一. 从1947年开始，提森-博内米萨男爵夫人的收藏品不再对公众开放。二. 这幅画受到了不专业的修复，涂上的颜料和修复细节将原画形象歪曲。最后重要的第三点是，大部分作者已将关注从鉴赏转移到了勃鲁格尔杰作中的符号意义和他的作品的文化历史地位。焦点落在了各大博物馆收藏品中他最出名的几幅画。毋庸置疑，这些原因正是为什么对历史学和符号学同样关注的佛利兹·格罗斯曼在1955年的专著中对这幅画只字不提[11]。布鲁塞尔皇家艺术馆的馆长菲利普·罗伯特-琼斯也将这幅画定义为‘前期归因’[12]。这其中例外的是弗里德兰德的调研成果《早期荷兰绘画》的英文版本，保持了先前的结论[13]。还有鲁汶天主教大学的教授华伦廷·德尼斯（鲁汶1916-1980年），波恩大学的讲师皮埃罗·比安科尼（米努西奥1899-1984年），都在他们的汇编中肯定了弗里德兰德对老彼得·勃鲁格尔的归因[14]。

几十年以后，在一个男爵夫人的本提克-博内米萨部分收藏品的巡回展中，这幅画于1986-87年间再次向大批公众展示，并以老彼得·勃鲁格尔署名。展览所到之地有洛桑的冬宫博物馆；巴黎的玛魔丹美术馆；东京的熊本-富山-宫城县；布鲁塞尔的美艺厅（本文作者首次在这里观赏到这幅画），和卢森堡的国家博物馆[15]。

在男爵夫人死后，她的收藏品被拍卖。当时这幅画的状况如此糟糕，无人能够识别它的原创者。近期对老彼得·勃鲁格尔的研究作者也无人提起这幅画[16]。就算他们知道它的存在，也只是通过那可悲的现状，或是弗里德兰德的黑白照片。

如今《圣塞巴斯蒂安市集上跳舞的农民》被清洁和修复，它重新绽放原有绘画的光彩，使鉴定也更加容易。正如前面提到的，这幅画的构图与勃鲁格尔的《霍博肯的集市》（藏于伦敦柯陶德艺术学院）画幅左面的一组群像非常相近。把这组群像放大，将旅店与整幅画水平平行，勃鲁格尔达到了一个清晰明了的构图。这个构图也用于他后期1567-1569年间创作的小一些的绘画表现形式。

对所用材料种类的科学性分析以及对它们使用方式的观察证实与老勃鲁格尔的每一个风格特征相对应。橡木以典型的斜边木条将画板分成四格，用暗销对接。接下来，画板被刷上方解石与动物胶水混合的液体。与对大部分勃鲁格尔的画作分析结果一样，这幅画也有一个棕色赭石色的首肯印记，混有一些铅白和炭黑。

画的底稿肉眼无法看见，即使在红外线照射下也很难辨别。就像其他许多勃鲁格尔的绘画一样，它最可能先是描绘一张1:1的草图，然后用液体颜料加强线条，很可能用的是黑色的炭质墨水。底稿建立了大多数人物的线条，建筑和其他构图元素。最后，测试出的色彩元素与勃鲁格尔其他绘画作品中的用色相呼应。

虽然可以说大部分材料都是运用在十六世纪后半叶的其他佛兰德绘画中，它们独殊的使用方式却是不同寻常的。以带斜边的木框来建画板，还有用1:1的草图来将一幅创作转移到木支架上，都十分特别。到目前为止，这些特殊的手法只有在老彼得·勃鲁格尔的绘画中才能见到。

很显然，这种特殊性同样表现在对颜料的使用上——少量，快速，一次性直接完成。在最后的完成作品中，流动的底色扮演了关键的角色。一块块色调差异较大的涂色区域正是勃鲁格尔具有代表性的绘画技巧。与和他同时期的画家技法相比，我们觉得将他的技法用一个现代名词‘超前’形容非常确切。

大部分勃鲁格尔的人物——男性，女性，儿童——经常是圆润的体型，面部和其他主要特征就像在他所有的绘画中一样，很容易识别。同样，背景中的人物将观赏者的视线吸引到构图，也是非常特别，可以毫不犹豫地被看作是勃鲁格尔的标志手法。画中人物栩栩如生，生动如真。那些粗俗的农民优雅地摆动，只有在老彼得·勃鲁格尔的笔下才能表现出来，任何一个他的复制者都无法做到。《圣塞巴斯蒂安市集上跳舞的农民》给我们提供了关于农民服装和其他物质文化的丰富信息，绘画手法与他的其他作品完全一样。

总结来说，从第一次出现在公众眼前，《圣塞巴斯蒂安市集上跳舞的农民》就被认为是老彼得·勃鲁格尔的作品。持有这个看法的包括早期佛兰德绘画的鉴赏大师麦克斯·弗里德兰德。 但是，当这幅画成为本提克-提森-博内米萨男爵夫人的收藏品之后，学者对它的兴趣渐渐消减。当几十年后重新出现在艺术品市场是，它带着严重的修补痕迹，艺术价值再也无法被欣赏。直到最近精确的修复，对材料科学性的检验，和对绘画技巧和风格新的评估，才最终将这幅画回归西方艺术历史的大师——老彼得·勃鲁格尔。

[1] Lichtert 2015.

[2] Van Mander (Miedema 出版社)， 1994-1997.

[3] 写有 ‘Sotheby / P. Cassirer / V.[on] Ruhemann / V.1929 / Attest / cf. Salomonsohn, / Berlin / B / Thyssen / VIII. 29’.

[4] Friedländer 1937, 60, no. 32.

[5] Michel 1931, 80.

[6] Glück 1931, no. 73. 他在第二本书 Glück （1951 年出版，no. 88）中重复了他的意见。

[7] Tolnay 1935, 97, no. 60.

[8] 关于托尔尼、请参考Dictionary of Art Historians 中关于L. Sorensen 的词条（Charles de Tolnay 出版）. 2018年8月6日搜索的http://www.arthistorians.info/tolnayc

[9] Heinemann 1937, vol. I, no. 62.

[10] Jedlicka 1938, 540.

[11] Grossmann 1955.

[12] Roberts-Jones 1969, 99,。同见于新版Roberts-Jones 1997, 328.

[13] Friedländer, 45, no. 33, pl. 41.

[14] Denis 1952, 34; Bianconi 1969, 105, no. 43 (1565?).

[15] La Collection Bentinck-Thyssen, 1986 – 87, no. 8.

[16] Marijnissen 和 Ruyffelaere （1988年）, Sellink （2006年）, 以及Silver （2011年）均未提及。唯一对此仍然做评价的是 Klaus Ertz 在他关于彼得·勃鲁格尔二世的专著中。他反对了格鲁克的观点，称这幅画并非其子所作 (Ertz 2000, I, 289, vol. II, 913, cat. no. A1277)。

Jacket

PIETER BRUEGEL THE ELDER
DANCING PEASANTS AT A ST. SEBASTIAN'S KERMIS
detail, oil on panel, private collection © UGent, Gicas, 2018

PIETER BRUEGEL I,
THE ARTIST AND THE CONNOISSEUR,
pen in brown ink on paper. Vienna, the Albertina Museum.
© the Albertina Museum Vienna

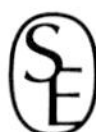

Silvana Editoriale

Direction
Dario Cimorelli

Art Director
Giacomo Merli

Editorial Coordinator
Sergio Di Stefano

Copy Editor
Clelia Palmese

Layout
Mirco Ameglio

Production Coordinator
Antonio Micelli

Editorial Assistant
Ondina Granato

Photo Editor
Alessandra Olivari, Silvia Sala

Press Office
Lidia Masolini, press@silvanaeditoriale.it

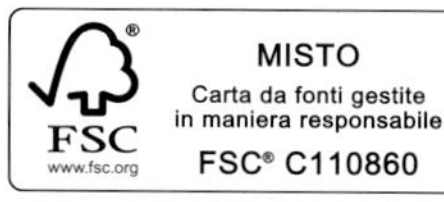

Silvana Editoriale S.p.A.
via dei Lavoratori, 78
20092 Cinisello Balsamo, Milano
tel. 02 453 951 01
fax 02 453 951 51
www.silvanaeditoriale.it

Reproductions, printing and binding
in Italy
Printed by Grafiche Aurora, Verona
December 2018